the yellow book

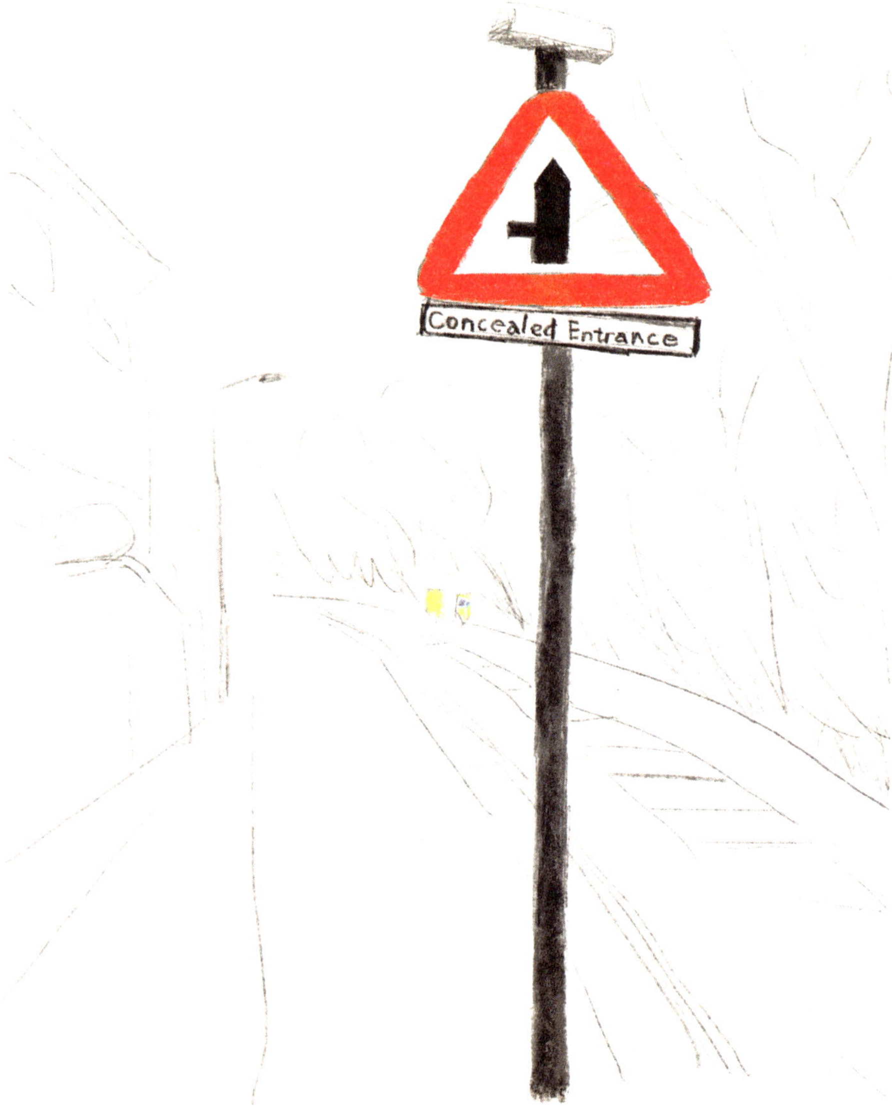

London, 2022

the yellow book

a traveller's diary

amitava kumar

HarperCollins *Publishers* India

First published in India by HarperCollins *Publishers* 2024
4th Floor, Tower A, Building No. 10, DLF Cyber City,
DLF Phase II, Gurugram, Haryana - 122002
www.harpercollins.co.in

2 4 6 8 10 9 7 5 3 1

P-ISBN: 9789356996021
E-ISBN: 9789356996038

Design by Gavin Morris
Printed and bound at Nutech Print Services - India

In memoriam
Shri I.C. Kumar (1935–2023)

What does the world look like? I don't think it looks like photographs. You have to find out for yourself, you have to draw it.

— David Hockney

CONTENTS

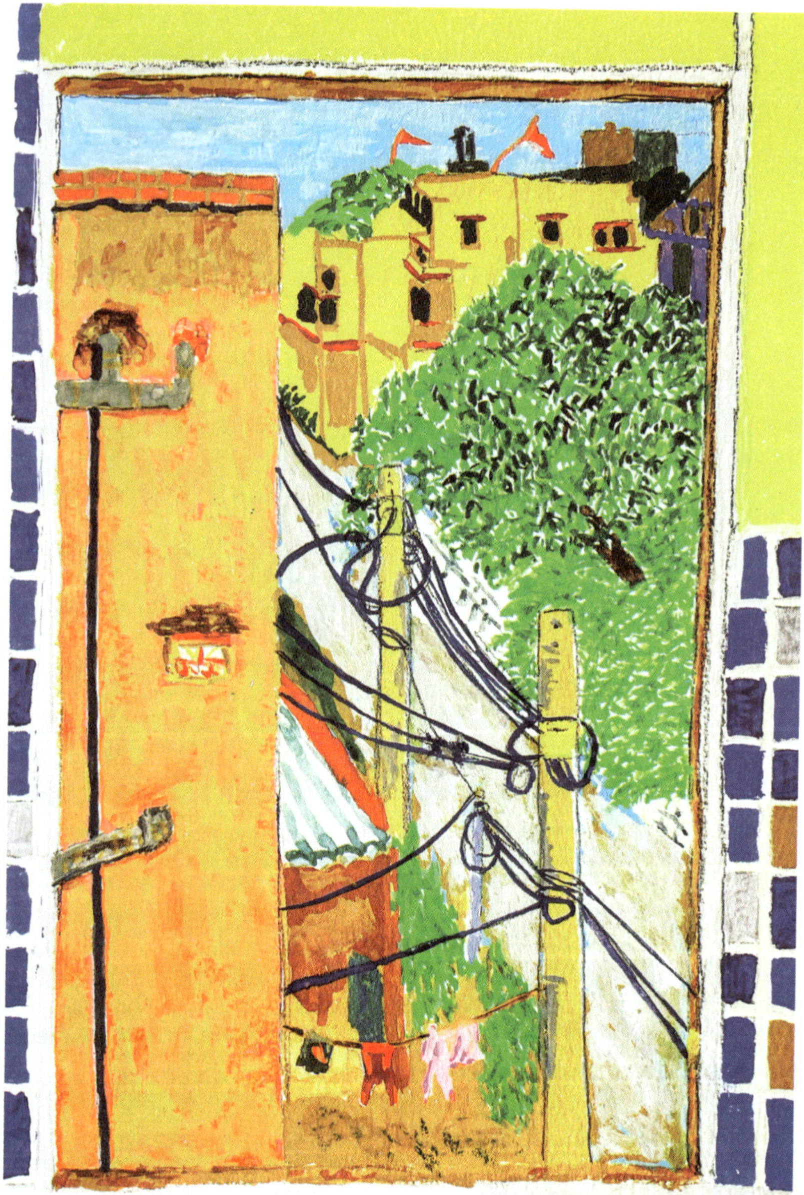

Below My Sister's Kitchen, Patna, 2022

Introduction

I have often wondered how writers arrive at titles for their books.

For me, a title for anything I am writing has almost always appeared accidentally. I mention this only because I want to underline the fact that art involves waiting. It requires a practice that cultivates an openness to possibility. Or, if you want to make it sound rigorous, a discipline of receptiveness. And then, what is wished for makes its magical advent.

More than a decade and half ago, I was writing my first novel, *Home Products*. Just as in many Hindi films I had watched during my childhood, there were two brothers in my story. The two were actually first cousins who had been brought up as brothers in Patna. One was Binod who was sincere and high-minded and wanted to be a writer. The other was Rabinder who had been in and out of trouble, a spirited man with an appetite for life. One day, by sheer chance, while taking a break from writing, I happened to pick up a book by Mark Twain and came across the following lines:

> Necessarily we are all fond of murders, scandals, swindles, robberies, explosions, collisions, and all such things, when we know the people, and when they are neighbors and friends, but when they are strangers we do not get any pleasure out of them, as a rule. … I

> would not give the assassination of one personal friend for a whole massacre of those others. And, to my mind, one relative or neighbor mixed up in a scandal is more interesting than a whole Sodom and Gomorrah of outlanders gone rotten. Give me the home product every time.

Give me the home product every time. There was a clue to my title! It seemed right for a novel about life in Bihar: my own first cousin had been arrested following a charge of kidnapping. There was also another thing to consider. I knew of mangoes, tea or textiles made for export only; this seemed true even of some Indian novels I had read. I wanted to write a novel in English that would strike the reader, especially a reader from north India, as a novel that could have been written in a language like Hindi. *Home Products* appealed to me because it seemed to capture not just the story but the kind of object I wanted to put in the literary marketplace.

Another novel of mine is *Immigrant, Montana*. The story of how that title came to me is older and even stranger. About twenty-five years ago, I was in my kitchen in Florida, listening to National Public Radio. Liane Hansen, on her show *Weekend Edition*, said that a wolf with a taste for sheep had been shot near Immigrant, Montana. A few days later I wrote a short story which, while telling the story of a couple in love, also told the story of 'the wolf running through sixty miles of undergrowth, across frozen lakes he had never seen before, never pausing because his eyes are hungry for home, for the sight of the familiar fence and the sheep ranged inside.' I had been writing about border-crossers and was working on a book called *Passport Photos*, but I decided I would visit Immigrant, Montana. The opportunity didn't come till almost a decade later. The Democratic Party convention was going to be held in Denver, Colorado. It was a historic event. Barack Obama was to become the first Black candidate to accept the nomination for the office of the President of the United States. A newspaper asked me to go to the convention to report from Denver. I was excited but a part of my excitement came from looking at the map and seeing that Montana was just north of Colorado. But the map also showed that I had made a mistake. I had misheard Hansen on the radio. The actual name of the place was Emigrant, Montana. After the Democratic convention, I drove there from Denver and found it a pretty but uninteresting place. A few years later when I began work on a novel about a young man from India who comes to the US and hears Dr Ruth on the radio, I decided I would title the book *Immigrant, Montana*. So much of our lives, especially immigrant lives, is about encounters with language, its distortions and reshapings. I decided I would stick with the name I had misheard. I was showing trust in the accidental.

I cannot recall precisely when it became clear to me that the book I published in January 2022 would be called *The Blue Book*—but I do know when I realized the sequel, the book you are holding in your hands, would be *The Yellow Book*. The name for the former had come from a set of associations. In school in Patna, we received our evaluations from our teachers in thin booklets called, 'blue books'. That term was buried in my memory. At the college where I teach, students write their test answers in blue books. A friend also made a playlist with that name. And when I painted a panel for an article on books, I chose to paint the book blue. I called the drawing *The Blue Book* and attached it in my mind to a story that V.S. Naipaul had once offered about the first sentence of Stephen Crane's 'The Blue Hotel': 'The Palace Hotel at Fort Romper was painted a light blue, a shade that is on the legs of a kind of heron, causing the bird to declare its position against any background.' A set of associations, once again near-accidental, made 'The Blue Book' an appealing title for me.

And then, in the fall of 2021, after I had made the final changes on the edited copy of *The Blue Book* and sent it away to the publishers, I would wonder from time to time if there was any chance of my publishing a second volume of journal entries and drawings. I hadn't, after all, stopped drawing. I had maintained a daily practice of writing in my diaries. Just as the semester was coming to a close, my friend and colleague Shane Slattery-Quintanilla asked me to come and speak to his class on creativity. Shane had many gifts for me, including two journals bound together. One journal was blue, and the other was yellow. Each student in that class had the same set of two journals. The blue journal was for writing one's own thoughts, and the yellow journal was for noting down other people's words. You liked a quote by Nietzsche, you put it in the yellow journal. If you had a thought of your own, you put it in the blue journal. Right then and there, holding my new journals in front of the class, I told the students that I had found the title for my next book of drawings and diary entries.

The first entry I made in my new journal that night was 'Decided that my next drawing book will be called *The Yellow Book*.' It was as if the universe had given me a gift. I had been doing the work all along but now, very quickly, the book had become a concrete idea. The following day I began drawing up a table of contents. In the weeks and months that followed, it wasn't simply that I was compiling what had already been done; instead, the idea of the book that had now become real in my mind made me alert and active. I wanted to explore the world and its colours.

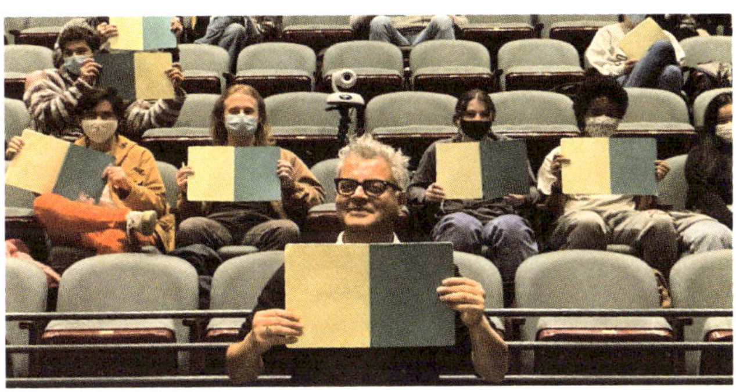

John, I think about the patch of light on the wall and how you painted it yellow. (I also think of Alice in her cradle.) The yellow you painted is like a name you gave to the light, no? No color represents light. Light would vote for none. Or maybe for black—because black, by opposition, really makes me imagine light. However, the yellow is a beautiful name, high up on the wall.

— John Berger, in a letter to John Christie. Quincy, 28 December 1997

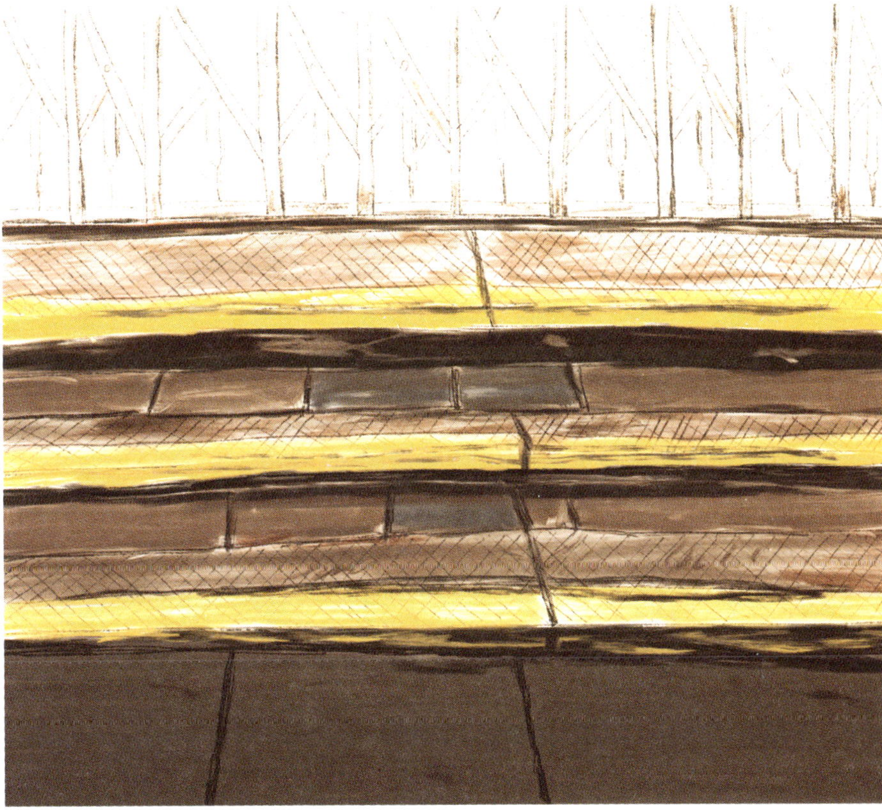

Steps Leading to the Shuttered Tube Station, London, 2022

How to Stop Time

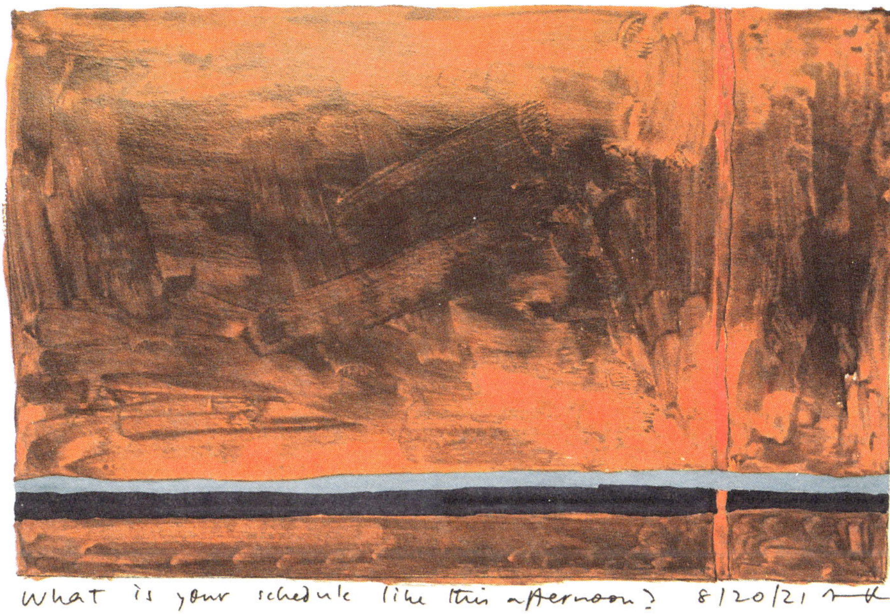

Poughkeepsie, New York, 2021

I must try to set aside half an hour in some part of my day, and consecrate it to diary writing. Give it a name and a place, and then perhaps, such is the human mind, I shall come to think of it a duty, and disregard other duties for it.
— Virginia Woolf

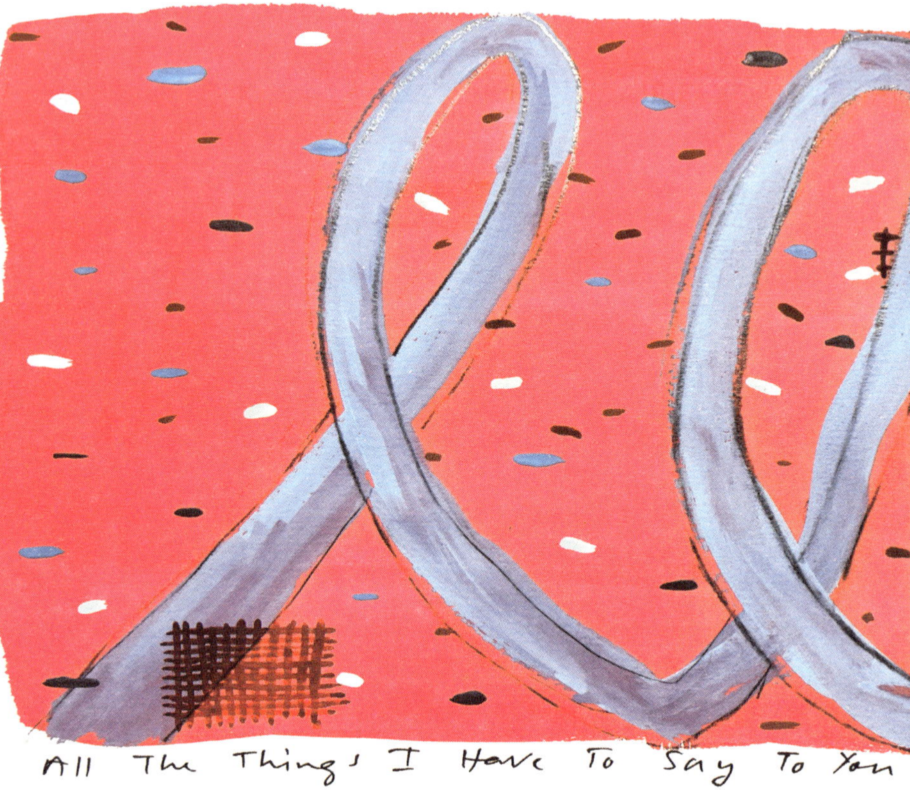

One. *How to stop time? You must keep a journal.* Your days will no longer be dull or ordinary again. This is the cardinal rule for artists and writers. This could also be turned into a fashion advice: try to own a thin jacket that can be worn even in warm weather, and in its inside pocket always keep a small notebook and a pencil.

I have found this fashion requirement to be a challenge in India. But there is a photograph of V.S. Naipaul from when he was working on *India:*

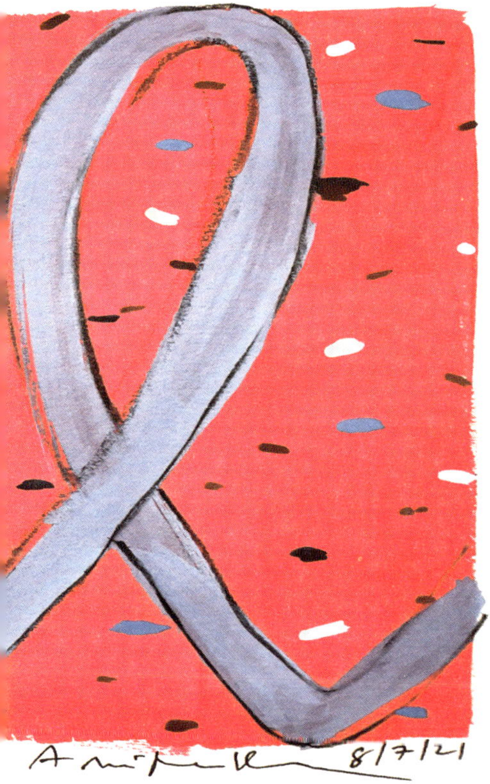

Poughkeepsie, New York, 2021

A Million Mutinies Now. From the glare in the photograph, you can feel the heat of the summer in Mumbai. A handkerchief lies on Naipaul's head as a protection from the sun. Heavy dark glasses shade his eyes. The writer is focused, taking notes. That small notebook in his hand will soon return to the inside pocket of his stylish cotton jacket. Naipaul was a fastidious note-taker, often asking people to repeat what they had said. I remember him whenever I'm too tired or lazy, and I also always remember that jacket.

Two. *Don't just keep a daily journal: make marks in your journal all the time.* For years, I had thought it was enough to note at the end of the day what had happened. That was useful, yes, but quite inadequate. Now, I believe a more intense practice is required for a richer life. I keep a set of journals handy. One journal is simply for free writing in the morning: that is the first thing I do, the morning pages, for ten or fifteen minutes. I also have different journals for the main writing project I'm working on. And then there is the file I have on my computer where I record the day's main events in brief. This is always done at night before I go to bed. But the most important journal I keep is the daily planner in which I note down how time is passing. I often write down how a particular half-hour was spent. More often, what I mark is an hour or a longer chunk of time, a long line crossing out three hours or more if I have been teaching. (The planner I use assumes I sleep between 10.30 p.m. and 6 a.m., which aren't exactly my hours, but no, I don't ever record my sleep.) I have been maintaining this practice of making notes in the planner for three years now. It has given me a degree of control over my life. And I have become an advocate of the morning pages because they make me feel less blocked. I recommend both. What I do not recommend is choosing something unusual and extreme, like a man named

Amar Bharati, Poughkeepsie, New York, 2020

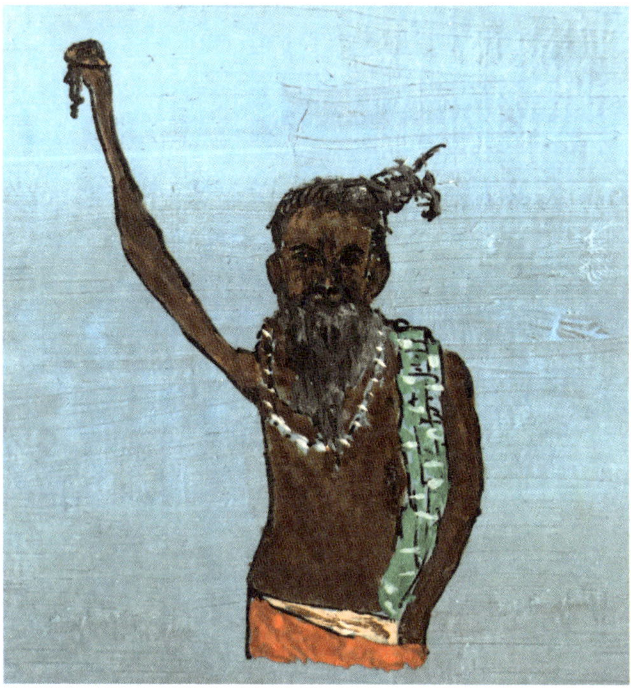

Amar Bharati who decided in 1973 to keep his right arm raised to show his dedication to Lord Shiva and hasn't lowered it since. His is a true story but I read about it first in a French novel.

Three. *Return to what you once enjoyed.*
A young woman named Eileen writes in an email to her friend Alice that some years earlier, when she was twenty-three, she had kept a diary which she called 'the life book'. She had begun by making a short daily entry, 'just a line or two, describing something good'. But then Eileen made a discovery. She recognized that she would sometimes do things 'for the purpose of putting them in the book, like taking a bath or going for a walk'. Eileen isn't a real person. She is a character in Sally Rooney's novel *Beautiful World, Where Are You*. I loved Eileen's insight about journalling and shared it with my students. I wanted them to learn from Eileen. Eileen's desire for doing something 'good' so that she could write a line about it in her book was wonderful: it showed that journalling is generative. A journal isn't simply a place for recording experiences; instead, it can be a way of *producing* experiences. I also liked Eileen's observation that when she went back and read those entries from six years earlier she remembered how she had felt, what she had seen or noticed or heard. 'There was something delicate about living like that—like I was an instrument and the world touched me and reverberated inside me.' When Eileen ruefully recalls those days, you cannot but feel a little sad for her. And urge her to resume journalling!

Clematis,
Poughkeepsie,
New York, 2021

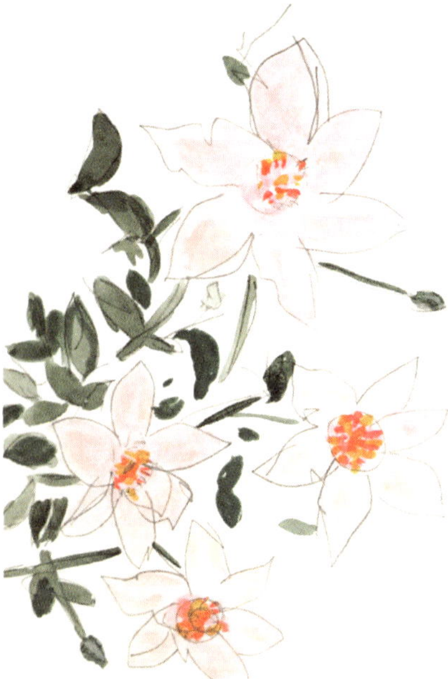

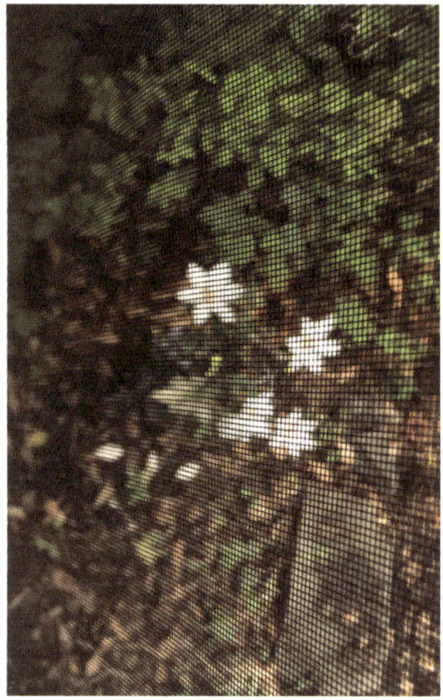

Four. *Be alert to the passing seasons. Time cannot be stopped, of course, but it can be lived more fully.*
I had always welcomed the arrival of spring by pasting a petal in my writing journal. But now I also paint the first signs of spring.

When he was still on Twitter, my friend Teju used to invite his followers to post their #flowerreport each Sunday. A collective journal of joy! Flowerespondents from all the world over: if you want to find cheer, just google the flower reports to witness the extraordinary beauty of this world.

For a few days each April, the cherry tree in the parking lot of our neighbourhood store in Poughkeepsie is covered with flowers and by now I have painted that tree more than once. Do you also have a favourite tree?

Poughkeepsie, New York, 2021

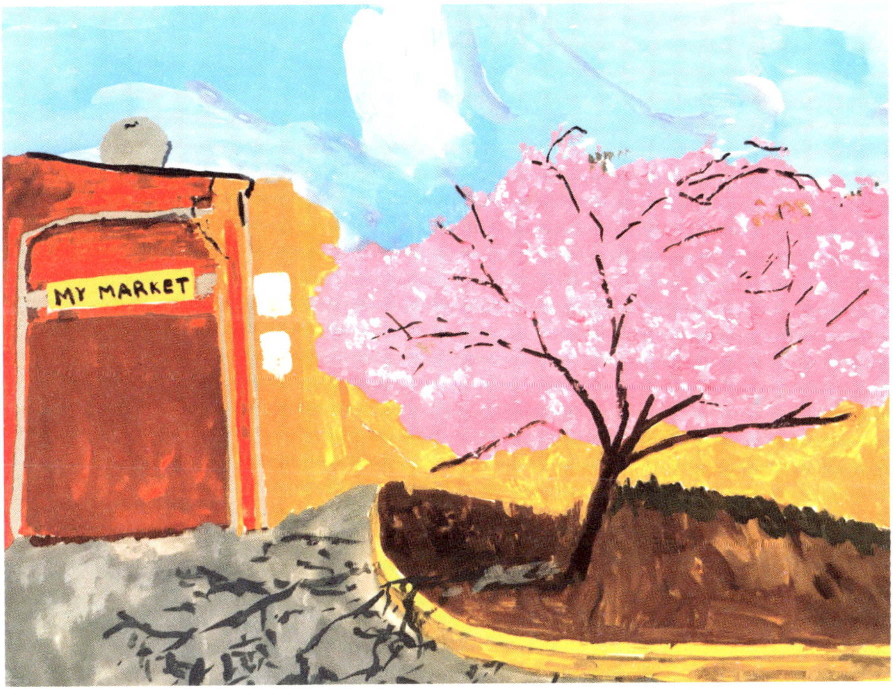

Five. *Not just the spring. Frozen winters too.* If you are an artist, even what causes you pain is material. Write or paint everything. I am primarily a writer but I find a great delight in painting because it so immediate and sensual. I started painting almost daily during the pandemic. There are some words by Maxine Hong Kingston that I came across during this time and have held close to me. This is what Kingston wrote: 'In a time of destruction, create something. A poem. A parade. A community. A school. A vow. A moral principle. One peaceful moment.'

Creek after Snowstorm, Poughkeepsie, New York, 2021

Six. *Time doesn't stop, nor do people. As with the seasons, everyone around you is changing. Observe them.*
So much of my painstaking journalling has revolved around the lives of my children. You must make a

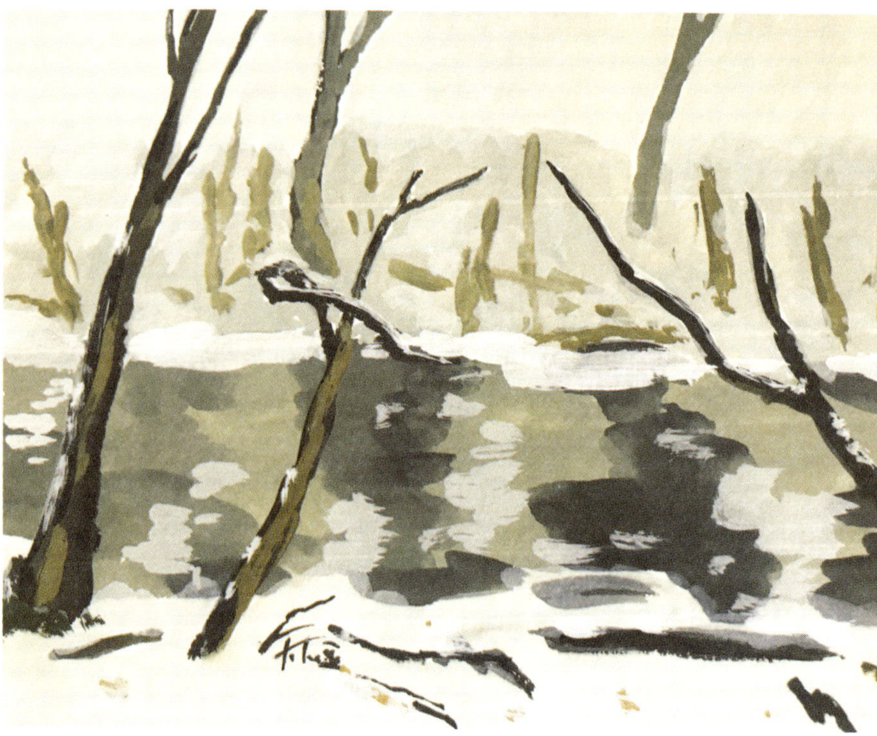

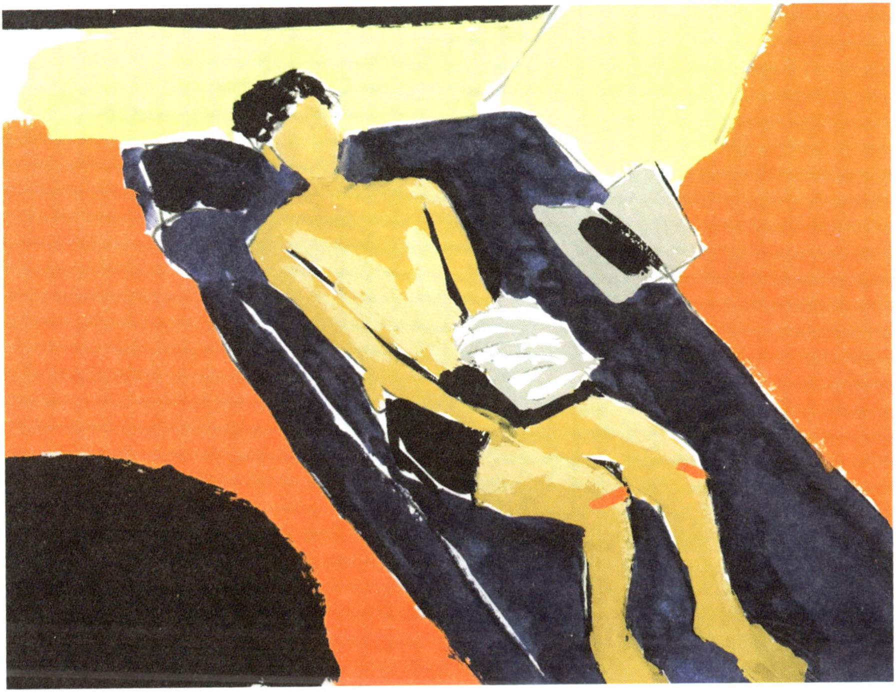

Rahul, Plus Band -Aids and Icepack, Poughkeepsie, New York, 2021

record because the mind forgets, it forgets even what is closest to it. One memory supplants another—and the earlier memory is gone forever.

P.S. If you have children, draw them. They will soon be grown-up and go on with their lives. As kids, they can be great models for amateur artists. Particularly when they are asleep. Or when they have fallen down and injured themselves and are unlikely to move because their arm is covered with an icepack.

Seven. *Read books. When we are reading, time stops. Or it doesn't weigh on us in the oppressive way it can when* *we are doing something we don't like.*

During the pandemic, Yiyun Li had this great idea that we should all form an online community to read *War and Peace*. I had never even tried to read that big book, but it became such a wonderful exercise, this practice of reading fifteen or twenty pages every day. It gave coherence to our days. The experience was so vital that A Public Space, the New York literary organization which had brought all of us readers together online, offered a whole list of other books in succession to be read as the pandemic stretched into the future. One of the books we read was W.G. Sebald's *The Emigrants* and I remember taking my family to the beach during the final week of reading. It was raining outside on the night when there was a virtual discussion about Sebald's profound and

Rain Sea, Montauk, New York, 2021

mournful novel. While the discussion was going on, I painted what I could see of the sea from my hotel balcony.

Eight. *Read more and more. (This is gimmicky but I like it when people repeat rules for emphasis.)*
When I think back to what Maxine Hong Kingston says about creating something during a time of destruction, I imagine forging a community of readers for this book you are holding in your hands. But I'd also like to advocate for other books. When my novel *A Time Outside This Time* was published, I was asked in an interview that if I were to open a bookstore, where would it be located and what my bestseller would be. I answered that we learn in the opening pages of *A Time Outside This Time* that our narrator is kicking back at a villa in Bellagio on Lake Como, Italy. He is there on a cushy fellowship. It had occurred to me that the little town of Bellagio needed a bookstore. I'd invite all the visiting fellows to do readings. The bestseller at the store? I told the interviewer that I had just re-read two William Maxwell novels, *They Came Like Swallows* and *So Long, See You Tomorrow*. I had found them so simple and piercing. In my bookstore, I would keep a stack of them on my checkout counter. People might buy a copy of, say, Cormac McCarthy's *Blood Meridian*, and I would pick up a copy of *So Long, See You Tomorrow*, and say, 'Have you read this by any chance? Can I offer a really strong recommendation?'

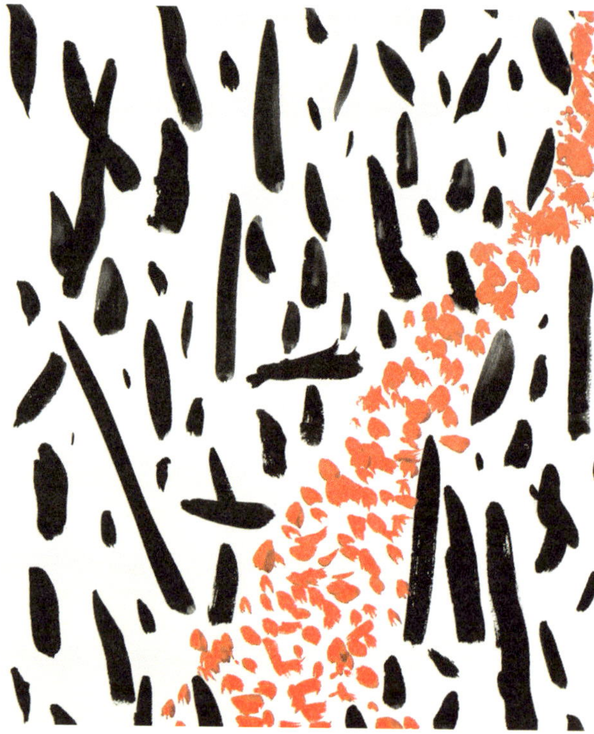

Under the Chuseok Moon, Poughkeepsie, New York, 2021

Nine. *Look at art.*

In late 2018, I needed to go to a physical therapist to get help on a knee injury. In the waiting room one day, I saw a copy of the *New York* magazine with a piece by Jerry Saltz titled 'How to Be an Artist'. I had begun painting by that time. In the piece, there were bits of advice for amateur artists: 'Carry a sketchbook with you at all times.' The pain in my injured knee was real, the exercises that the therapist made me do were sometimes excruciating, but for the ten days that I went there, I looked forward to reading the same magazine article over and over again. It was a great pleasure to look at a wide variety of art. That same repetitive act of looking at art and perusing advice about art-making seemed to me a way of stopping time. You can do it too by following good artists and galleries on Instagram. Looking at art, like writing daily or walking daily or drawing daily, is now a part of my everyday practice. I have learnt, for instance, that the cut-outs Matisse made late in life were a response to the restrictions born of old age. Matisse was going blind and unable to paint. Cutting was a new way to think about shape and colour and composition.

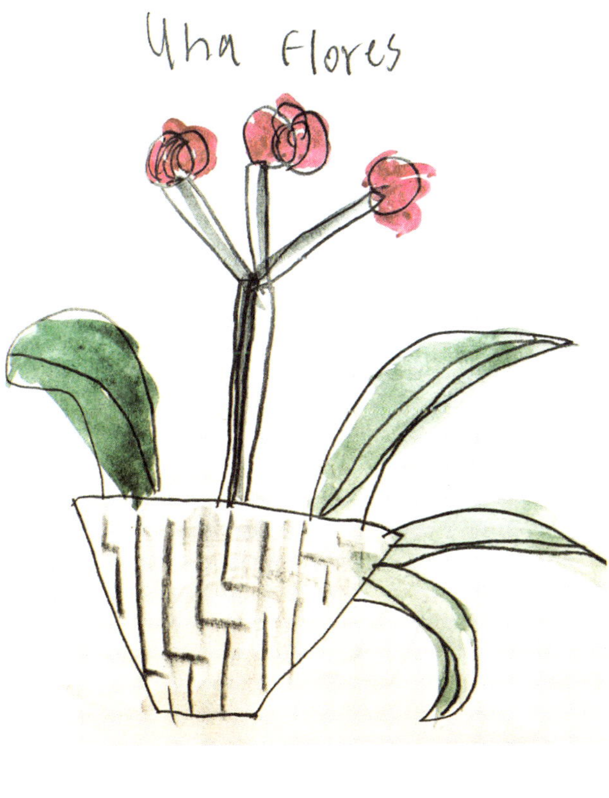

Rahul's Drawing, Poughkeepsie, New York, 2020

This makes me think of how, instead of hiding one's limitations, one ought to make use of them.

P.S. Jerry Saltz turned his article into a book and I bought it during the pandemic. My son, who was ten at that time, read the book with me. Here is a drawing he made of his mother's houseplant that I like very much.

Ten. *Write or draw or walk to save someone's life, even if the life you are saving is your own.*
Just before my students arrived in London from the US for a study abroad semester during the spring of 2022, I shared with them the first paragraph of a short book by the great German film-maker Werner Herzog. The book is titled *Of Walking in Ice*.

Here is the first sentence of the book: 'At the end of November 1974, a friend from Paris called and told me that Lotte Eisner was seriously ill and would probably die.' In simple, declarative sentences, Herzog writes that German cinema would not survive Eisner's death, and 'we would not permit her death'. He took a jacket (remember the jacket, always), a compass and a duffel bag. His boots were new, and he writes that he 'had confidence in them'. And then comes this sentence which I must quote in full: 'I set off on the most direct route to Paris, in full faith, believing that she would stay alive if I came on foot.'

What an extraordinary sentence. None of my students, during the entire semester that followed, referred in their journals to this passage from Herzog. And why should they? It is possible that the name Werner Herzog means nothing to them. Herzog is even older than their professor. More importantly, death isn't of interest to them. They are full of life themselves. And we, or at least I, can't grudge them that.

You will have to read Herzog's account to find out if he succeeded in his walk; what I want to convey right now is the clear and immediate sense of his belief and strength of purpose. Death is forever coming for us. Every tick of the clock brings it closer. Yes, death is coming. I have nothing but admiration for the way in which Herzog chose to stop time.

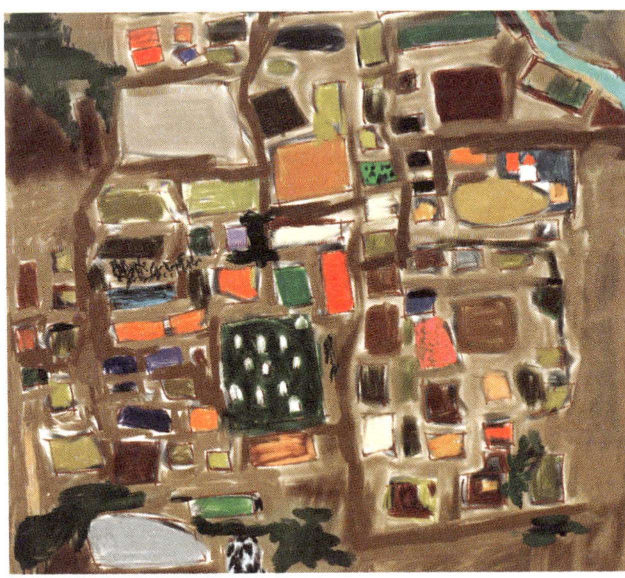

The Heart of the City / A Cemetery / Of Grief, London, 2022

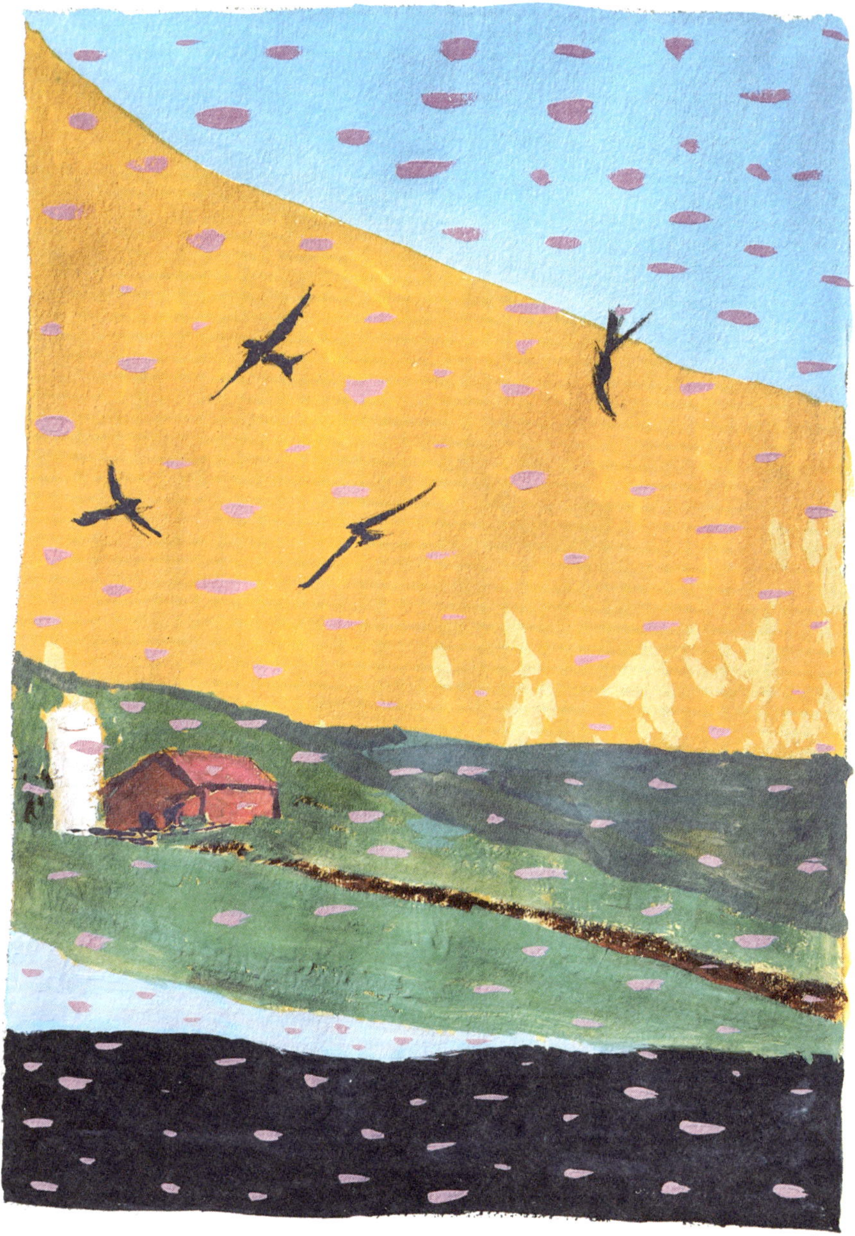

They Came Like Swallows

I don't particularly care for the drawing on the facing page. I didn't draw it from life, from any specific observation. Instead, it is a work of imagination, provoked by a reading of William Maxwell's heartbreaking 1937 novel, *They Came Like Swallows*. The title comes from a poem by W.B. Yeats, 'Coole Park, 1929'. I was reading the novel in August 2021 as a part of an online reading group. Maxwell was writing about the flu pandemic of 1918—his own mother had died from it. This death, which occurred in Maxwell's early childhood, haunted his life and so much of what he wrote.

My reading of the novel was haunted by something else: the Covid-19 pandemic that had abated by then but was by no means over. A few months earlier, in March, my elderly father had received his first dose of the vaccine in India. And a bit later, I got my first dose too. However, the second wave of Covid in India, particularly during the months of March and April 2021, had been utterly devastating. I didn't know of anyone whose family hadn't been affected; my own family members had suffered deaths. Why did my paintings about what was happening in India seem closer to me, somehow more real, even though they too were often painted from my imagination? It might be because of the intimacy of history: I was living through this pandemic and only reading about the

They Came Like Swallows, Poughkeepsie, New York, 2021

pandemic of 1918 from a huge distance in time. But there's also another reason. All the drawings I made in response to the news from India were driven by sorrow and rage. The reports said that the metal in the crematoriums would sometimes melt from the fires burning; that relatives were often unable to even participate in any ritual of farewell; that the Ganga

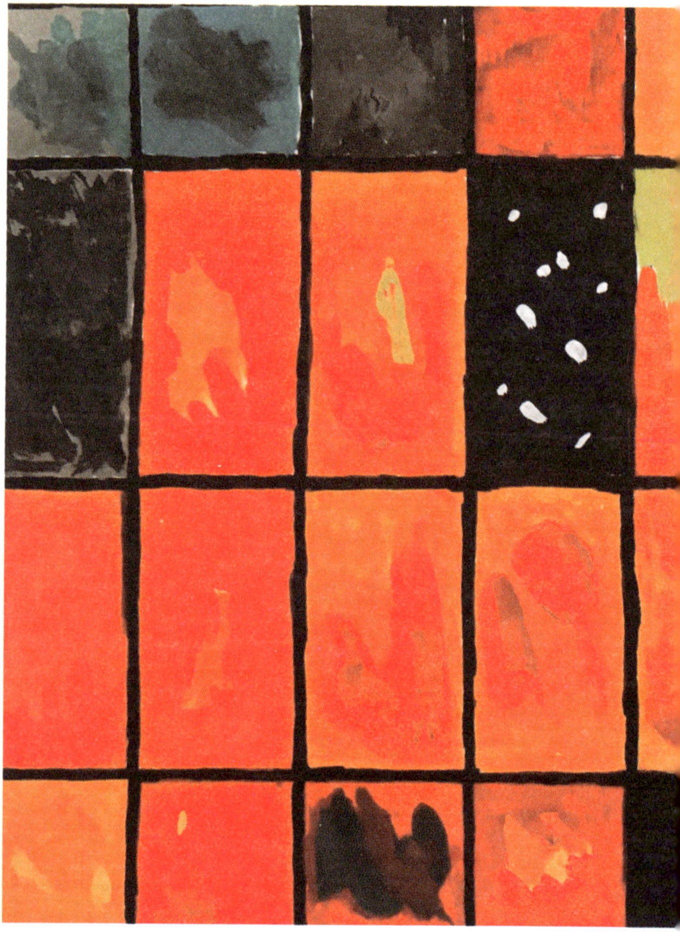

Too Many Hurried Goodbyes, Poughkeepsie, New York, 2021

upstream from Patna was choked with bodies and the poor, unable to afford cremations, were burying their dead on the riverbank. I painted in order to feel less helpless. And hiding in this despair was an even greater fear: that those in power, who had organized election rallies and religious gatherings and helped spread the virus were, in the future, going to spin this story of loss into a victory song. The chief minister of Uttar Pradesh warned that those talking of shortages of oxygen cylinders would be arrested. So I made an abstract painting called *Too Many Hurried Goodbyes*. This was on 25 April 2021 when I got news of the death of an uncle in Bhagalpur from Covid. When I was quite young, I would watch him swim across the broad breadth of the Ganga, his body becoming tiny in the distance, and then swimming back, making that impossible return to being life-sized again.

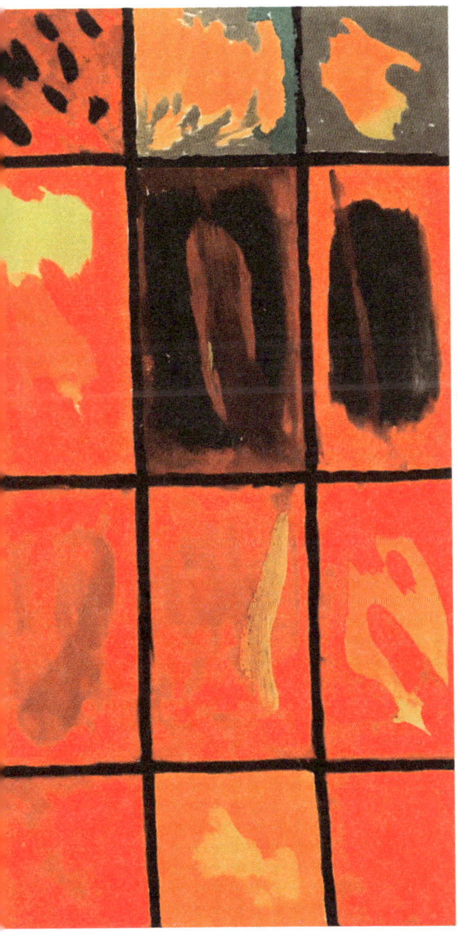

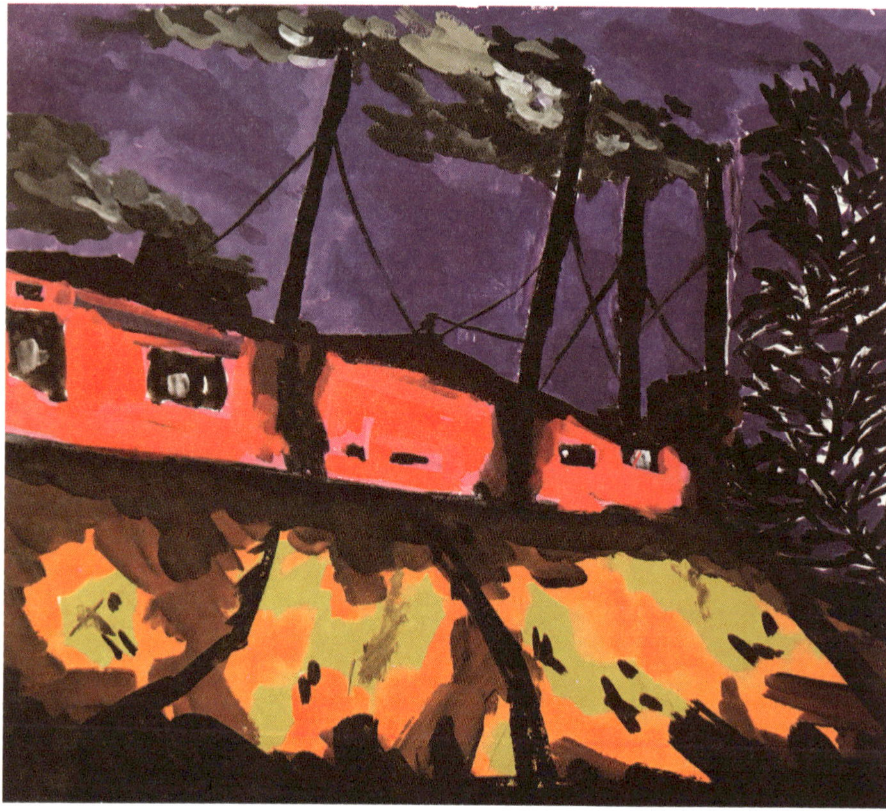

Fires Burning 24x7, Poughkeepsie, New York, 2021

Such devastation, so much grief. So many million dead worldwide, and hundreds of thousands dead in India. The staggering effects of this global catastrophe will be felt for a very long time; in fact, its real and far-reaching consequences, not just on our health and our psyches but also on the health of economic systems as well as systems of governance, will perhaps not be entirely clear to us for years. In the meantime, we must marvel at the fact that we have survived. Where the state failed, our neighbours helped. Our families and friends. Doctors and nurses. One night on TV I heard a historian say that authoritarian leaders in power lie all the time. These leaders will claim that it is their opponents and journalists instead who lie. Soon people don't know what to believe. They think there is no truth out there in the real world, and then the game is over. Democracy is dead. Such prognostications during the pandemic only heightened other anxieties already present like viruses in the air. What kept my sanity intact, and what helped keep at bay the overwhelming feeling of helplessness, was the ability to write and draw. I was keeping a record of all that was ugly and also all that I found beautiful.

Ganga Ghat, Poughkeepsie, New York, 2021

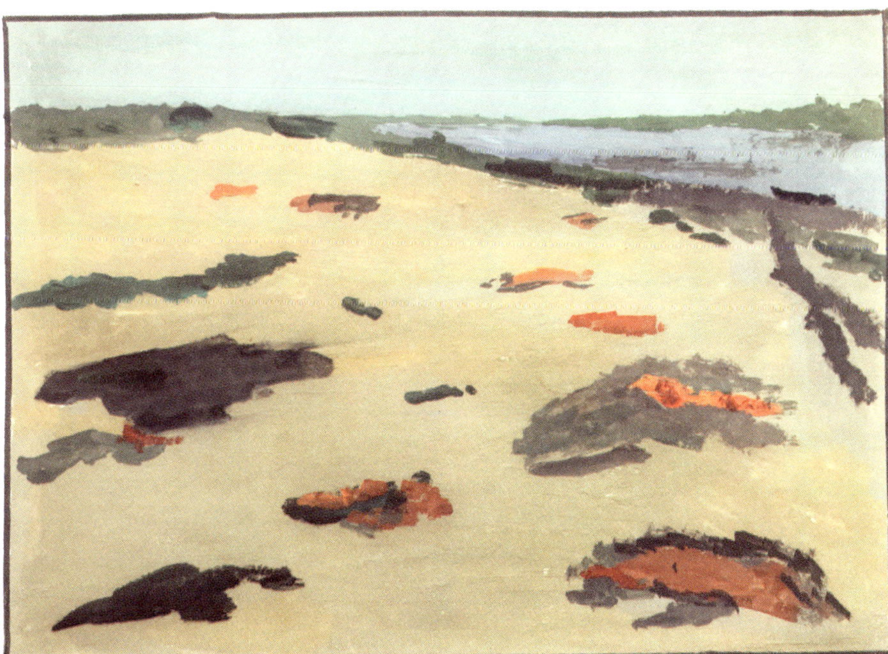

You Must Believe in Spring

For Hemali

The title for this section comes from an album by the jazz great Bill Evans. I had started doing drawings of plants and trees on the Hampstead Heath in London when I came across the Evans album on YouTube. The title spoke to me at different levels. It evoked for me the magnificent work of David Hockney during the lockdown. While sheltering in place in Normandy, Hockney had documented the arrival of spring, painting on his iPad the flowering lilies, refulgent greens and fruit trees bursting into bloom. (See Hockney's book *Spring Cannot Be Cancelled*.) One commentator had described Hockney's recent work as demonstrating 'the liberating power of creativity'. I was interested in that idea of creativity, particularly because the pandemic had forced me to think, on a personal and social level, of how to respond with imagination when confronted with a crisis. The title of the Evans album also spoke to my own experiences in the new city. I had come to London with students from my college in the winter of 2021-22 for a study-abroad semester. I was living with my wife and son in a small flat near the Hampstead Tube station. Before I had arrived in England a few weeks earlier, amidst the Omicron scare, I hadn't even been sure that my students would be able to join me. Yet here we were, wearing masks when we travelled on the London

Underground, but coming out on the street to walk to museums and places along the Thames. The uncertain days of winter were soon going to turn to spring. For a few days, my wife and I would look out of the window in our stairwell, and point out to each other, just beyond the sewer pipes, a pink rose blooming on a bush. And then, two weeks later, the bush was suddenly heavy with blossoms.

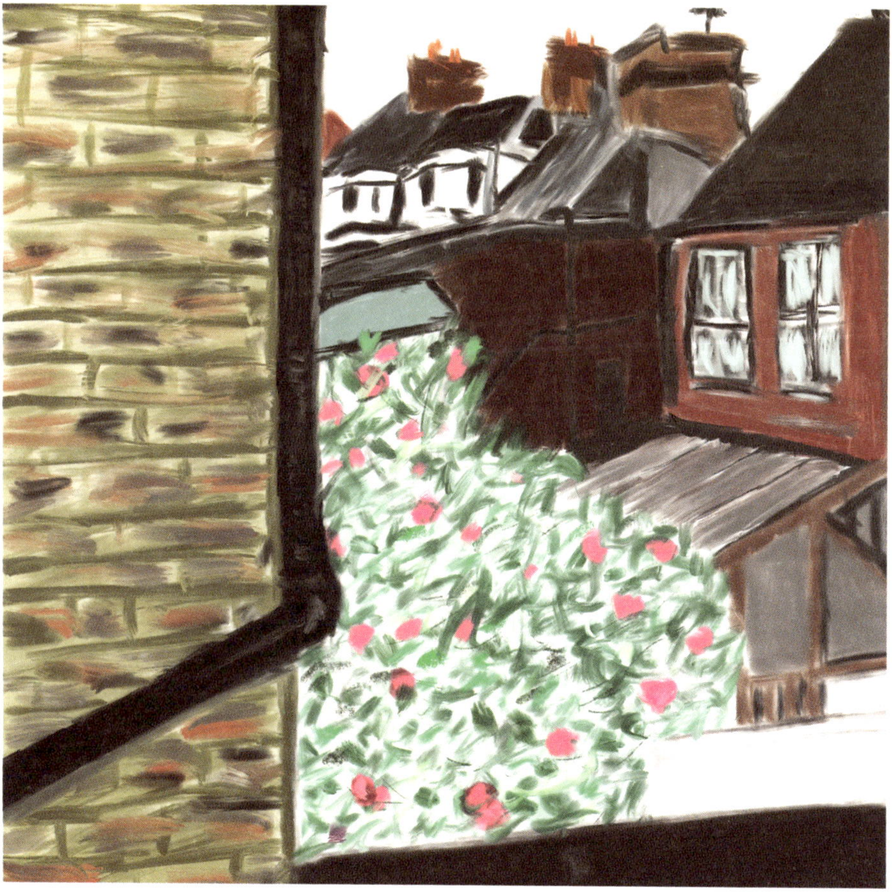

Stairwell, London, 2022

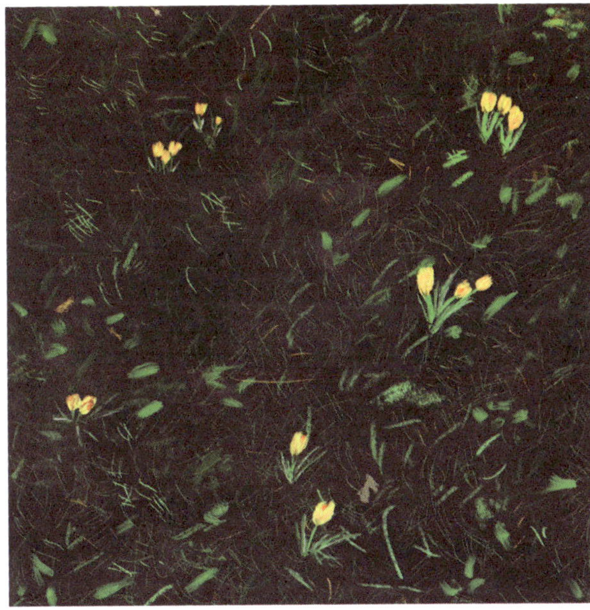

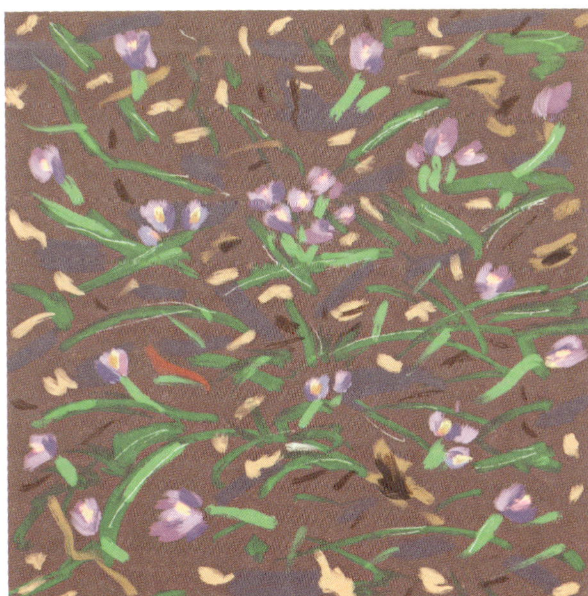

Crocuses,
London, 2022

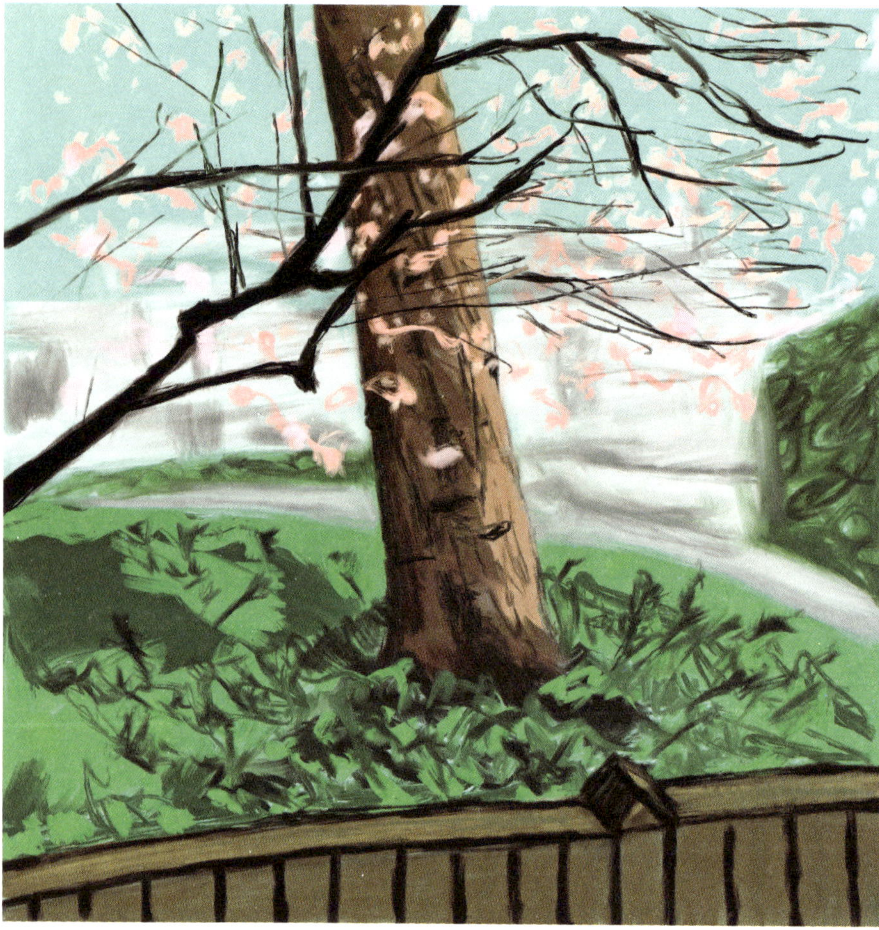

Keats House, London, 2022

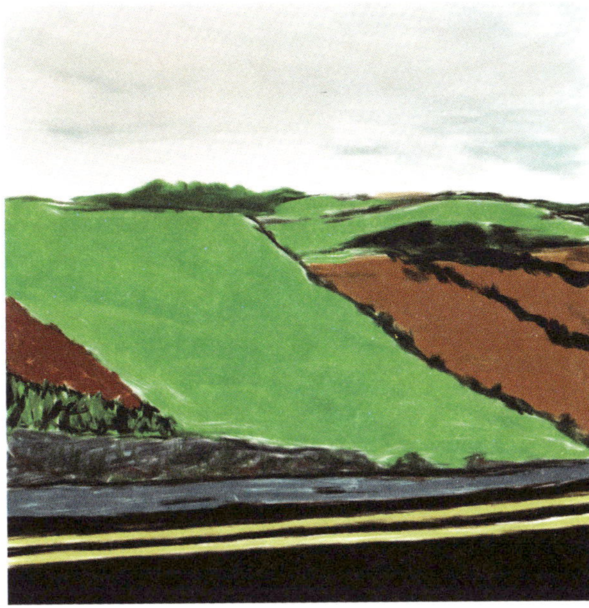

In the Middle of February,
Oxfordshire, 2022

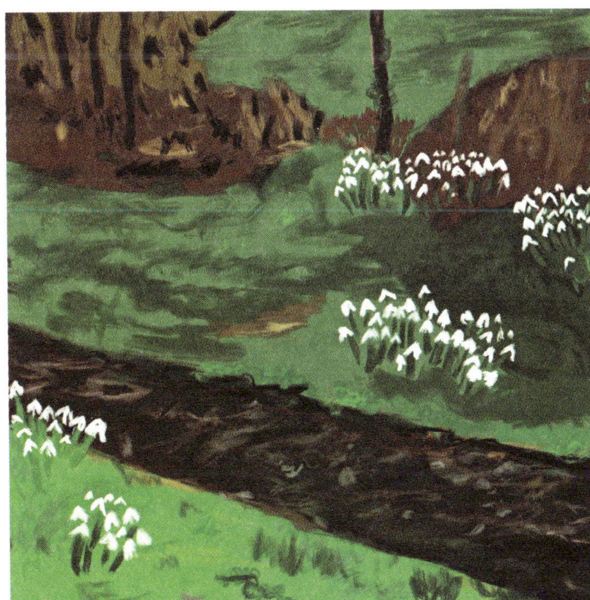

Voice Lessons

For Claire

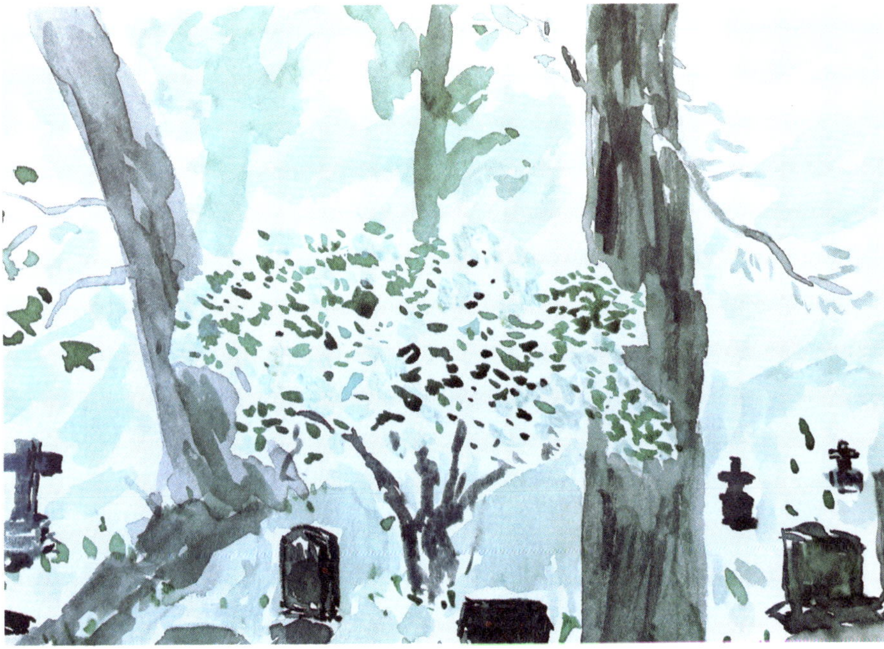

Cemetery, Georgia Avenue Sewanee, Tennessee, 2021

'Plots are for dead people', but voice—oh, voice is how you know you're alive.

Mars Blackmon, played by Spike Lee, in *She's Gotta Have It* saying, 'Please baby. Please baby. Please baby, please baby. Please, please. Baby, baby.' I had arrived in the US the same year the movie was released, in 1986; I was a new immigrant, a graduate student, when, soon after it came out, I watched *She's Gotta Have It*. The idea of language as excess. Language not just for writing academic papers. Language of desire but also language as desire. This was an early lesson about voice.

Years passed. I was producing academic essays and exercises in critical theory, and my writing had the consistency of freshly mixed cement. But I was dreaming of escape. There is a clipping from a newspaper that I stuck in a notebook—an exchange between a journalist and the literary agent David Godwin. The journalist asks Godwin what turns him on in a book, and the literary agent replies, 'Voice, not so much story.' Godwin says that he has been reading a book about a woman's childhood in Botswana. The first twenty pages are dull, and then there is a wonderful scene. 'Her grandfather is sitting on a veranda, surrounded by masks, drinking red wine. Two little red drops hang on his lips. Suddenly the masks come down, sit on his mouth in the half-light, sip, and speed away. You know that's where the book begins. It's so arresting, so different.'

Godwin wasn't my agent yet. But when I began writing something to show him, I thought, that's what I will do: something 'arresting' and 'different'. I wasn't worried that I didn't really have a plot ready; I'd have voice. What was I hoping to catch? I was hoping to avoid that hushed tone of TV commentators at Wimbledon—public but with a false intimacy—that is adopted a few moments before a difficult second serve: 'Venus has appeared frail, but she can summon an inner reserve. Let's see if she can do it here.' 'Seventh double fault. Her task will be uphill now.' This also meant I wouldn't have green grass or white lines or players in fashionable skirts. No strawberries and cream. I'm from the Hindi heartland, and I thought a prison would be rather nice.

My first cousin had been arrested and jailed around that time. The state of Bihar, where I'm from, was described then as having only one growth industry, kidnapping. A doctor, or a businessman, or their kid, would be kidnapped and a call would come for a ransom. One such call had been traced to my cousin's phone. My sister believed that the police had made a mistake. It is true that my cousin had suffered. I chose to believe that my cousin had suffered for literature. In that first novel, *Home Products*, my narrator, Binod, visits his cousin in prison. This cousin, Rabinder, is full of plans. He tells Binod that he would like to sell an idea to some big mobile phone company. It was an idea for a commercial, but Rabinder's real scheme was to get into film-making once he was out of prison.

The commercial would begin with a shot of a blue-green planet afloat in dark space. Then, with instant thousandfold magnification, the camera would digitally zoom into the part of the landmass in the northern hemisphere that lies above the Indian Ocean, the subcontinent flecked closer to the top of the screen by the white crest of a wave representing the Himalayan snow peaks. The camera would veer right, coming closer to the ground to reveal, for one five-hundredth of a second, the muddy expanse of the Ganges, then panning above it to a city visible only as a dirty wash of miniature rooftops, their colour a uniform grey. The camera's eye would pick out a large yellow building, the state's prison. There would be a short pan along the length of a tall wall before it paused at a barred room in which sat a solitary man. The film would cut to a shot from above: the top of the man's head and, pressed to his right ear, a mobile phone.

'What do you think?' Rabinder asks Binod.

Binod says that the idea is a good one but asks why the prison is necessary.

Rabinder says, 'Honestly, can you think of any place where a mobile phone would be more needed than in prison?'

My cousin was released from his jail cell; soon, he started building a luxury hotel. And David Godwin didn't take me on as a client for that book. That would happen later. I think I had mistaken a scene—the masks coming down from the wall to sip wine—as an example of voice. It was just a scene. A surprising scene, no doubt. So, too, the man in the prison cell. Voice is something else. Maybe the next novel I wrote had it, this element of voice, because Godwin decided

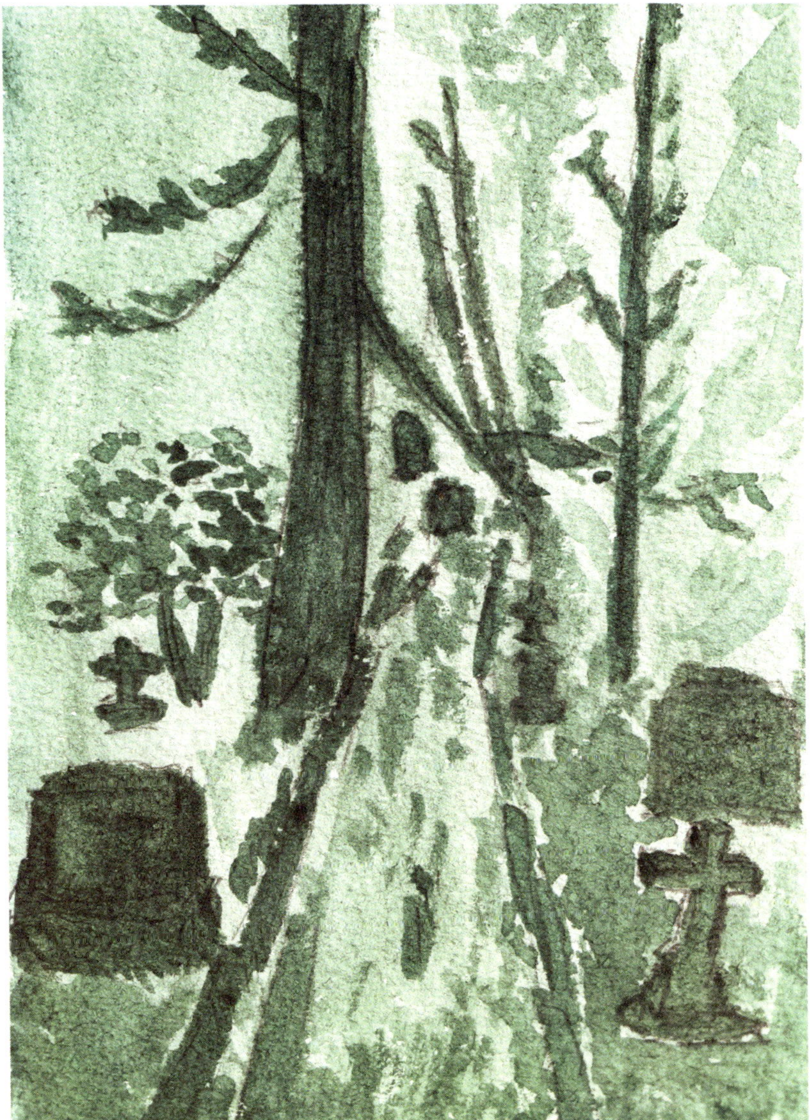

Cemetery, Georgia Avenue, Sewanee, Tennessee, 2021

to represent me and sold *Immigrant, Montana*. For this novel, I had picked up another lesson in voice.

I had read Vladimir Nabokov's memoir, *Speak, Memory*. Nabokov's writing was for me a wonderful example of a desirable voice for writing because it was alert to the fact that art is always also artifice. When I learnt later that he had published parts of *Speak, Memory* first as fiction in the *New Yorker*, I felt doubly delighted. I didn't for a moment think that he was being false or meretricious; instead, he was announcing that the text was fabricated, made up through labour and a love of words. This is the most honest thing a writer can do.

In Chapter 3 of *Speak, Memory*, Nabokov tells the reader about his distinguished family tree, his affluent ancestors and their role in history, their eccentricities, etc. At one point he talks about his mother's brother, his Uncle Ruka, who left his enormous wealth for Nabokov to inherit upon his death at the end of 1916. Of course, the revolution came and divided Nabokov from his inheritance. A lovely little description of the property follows before Nabokov breaks off and inserts a new section which is no more than ten lines. He directly addresses the reader: 'The following passage is not for the general reader, but for the particular idiot who, because he lost a fortune in some crash, thinks he understands me ...' More than anything else in the memoir it was this turn that demonstrated to me the writer-as-magician stepping out of the job of pulling rabbits out of hats and revealing the true magic, the secret of how it is all done. I carried this voice in my head for years and then sneaked it into *Immigrant, Montana*. Nabokov's sense of command, or maybe it was just his grasp of artistic freedom, also gave me permission to directly address my reader and take them into confidence. This was another lesson in voice. I included commentaries on my writing process and also pictures of clippings from my notebooks.

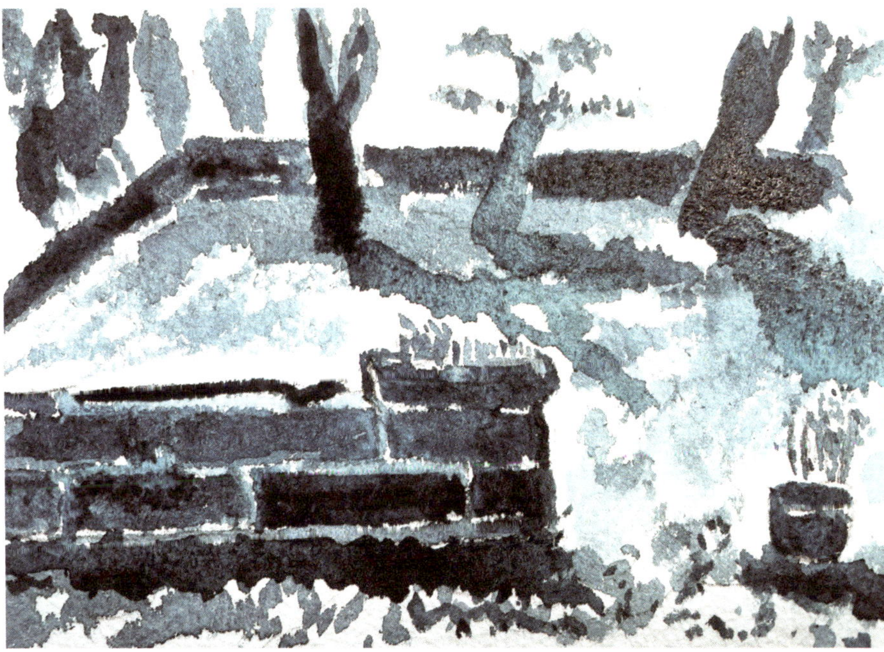

Cemetery, Georgia Avenue, Sewanee, Tennessee, 2021

In a 1997 interview for *BRICK* magazine, W.G. Sebald told James Wood the following:

> I think that fiction writing, which does not acknowledge the uncertainty of the narrator himself, is a form of imposture and which I find very, very difficult to take. Any form of authorial writing, where the narrator sets himself up as stagehand and director and judge and executor in a text, I find somehow unacceptable. I cannot bear to read books of this kind.

I am of the same view. So, the voice of a narrator struggling with truth, indicating with a pointed finger the joints in the scaffolding, is also mine. In a piece of fiction I'm working on right now, an Indian woman who works for CNN in Atlanta has this memory:

> I had become conscious that when we were in the company of educated people in Patna, my father would tell them that he was born in the same hospital as Orwell in Motihari. I later found out that Orwell was indeed born in the same sleepy town as my father, close to our ancestral village, Khewali, but it is quite likely that his mother had given birth in the small bungalow that served as the Orwell residence. Richard Blair, Orwell's father, was a sub-deputy opium agent for the British. The bungalow in which they had lived in Motihari, now a dilapidated cowshed overrun by pigs and stray

> dogs, was described recently in one Patna newspaper as an 'animal farm'.

The story that the woman is telling is very close to mine, except that I discovered Orwell when I came to Delhi on a scholarship to finish high school. His essay 'Why I Write' was a part of the assigned reading for our class. I'm mentioning Orwell now because the boldness, the freedom, the playfulness I see in Nabokov is far removed from Orwell's voice that I first associated with the voice of a writer.

Back in my late teens, when I read Orwell's essay, I didn't know that this famous writer had been born in Motihari. I identified with him chiefly because in his essay he described a voice in his head, 'a continuous "story" about myself, a sort of diary existing only in the mind', which was 'a mere description of what I was doing and the things I saw'. Orwell had written:

> For minutes at a time this kind of thing would be running through my head: 'He pushed the door open and entered the room. A yellow beam of sunlight, filtering through the muslin curtains, slanted on to the table, where a match-box, half-open, lay beside the inkpot. With his right hand in his pocket he moved across to the window. Down in the street a tortoiseshell cat was chasing a dead leaf,' etc. etc. This habit continued until I was about twenty-five, right through my non-literary years. Although I had to search, and did search, for the

right words, I seemed to be making this descriptive effort almost against my will, under a kind of compulsion from outside.

It is possible we all do this as children or adolescents and then grow out of the habit, unless you are a writer. In my case, I had become conscious of this activity after I began reading literary texts. Orwell was a part of that early education. I could be in a Delhi Transport Corporation bus in Daryaganj, and a voice running in my head would name the objects I saw being sold on the street, their colours, the look in the eyes of the sellers.

I also read Orwell's essay about the politics of the English language; he wanted to promote writing that was unfussy and modest, never calling attention to itself. He was, of course, giving voice to an ideology: post-war socialist, I imagine. When I first encountered that language, I wanted to make it my voice. It was also a part of my desire, as a postcolonial, to escape the colonial inheritance that dictated that our use of English ought to be, as Lord Macaulay had intended, the language of the clerks. My father wrote his letters to us in a stiff, bureaucratic language. My fondness for the Orwellian diction was challenged in the American graduate programmes in critical theory where I found myself writing sentences suffocated with defensive subordinate clauses. In my time since, especially in the writing of *Immigrant, Montana*, I have tried to embrace a voice that was not just loud, exaggerated, sexual, but also exuberant. In interviews, I would say that English had been taught to us as a language in which we had to do our homework; to write fiction or imaginative non-fiction was to sense a liberation in language.

The voice you own, or adopt, is to a large extent based on your education. Orwell was a part of my education. But that was long ago. When I think of voice now, pure voice in non-fiction, the richest, most enduring fabrication, the first thing that comes to mind are the interviews collected and shaped by Svetlana Alexievich. I also like that the voices collected in Claudia Rankine's *Citizen* came in response to a questionnaire shared on some listserv far removed. I've always wanted to know what the questions were. I admire Rankine's collaboration with sculptor Kate Clark to access what is uncanny and disturbing in our racialized existence. Or think of Janet Malcolm's 'Forty-One False Starts'. I have used that piece in my journalism classes a few times, but my main desire was to learn from it myself. How to have a voice that is provisional and probing, fragmentary and precise? I think my friend Teju Cole's essay on the 'Black Panther' attains that ideal in a satisfactory way.

It is often easy, as in this essay, to slip into memoir. I have a mild distrust of this voice: it is a distrust of the comfort that an easy access to the past offers. It is possible that I have on occasion tried to overcorrect this tendency. If you have ever read my essay 'Where Is Your White Literature Section?' you will know what I mean. At a friend's suggestion, I walked up to the counter at different bookshops in New York City one fine spring day and asked the salesperson there, 'Excuse me, where is your white literature section?' Over and over again, I posed this question to helpful sales staff who—bewildered, patient, clueless, condescending and, in one case, angry—tried to tell me what to buy. At McNally Jackson, the nice sales guy said, '*Who* are the great white authors?' Immediately to his right was the seeming answer. Withdrawing a copy of *Freedom* half an inch from its place on the shelf, he gently intoned, 'Franzen.' He also introduced me to other names, Hemingway, Cormac McCarthy, Philip Roth. In my essay, I talk of how wearying I found the exercise, not just what people said but the pretence I had to maintain throughout, this voice I had adopted as the Sacha Baron Cohen of American letters. I remember thinking to myself that I had dissembled, I had lied, and I would never be invited on *This American Life*. But that unstable place, where earnestness gives way to exploration and you have found a voice that is unsettling and maybe even disturbing and exhausting, is a place I want to visit again. I hope an enterprising and fun editor comes up with a compelling idea, or that inspiration strikes me at the right moment. I'd love to find out how English is spoken there and the voice in which I'd report from that place.

Outside Stirling's
Cafe, Sewanee,
Tennessee, 2021

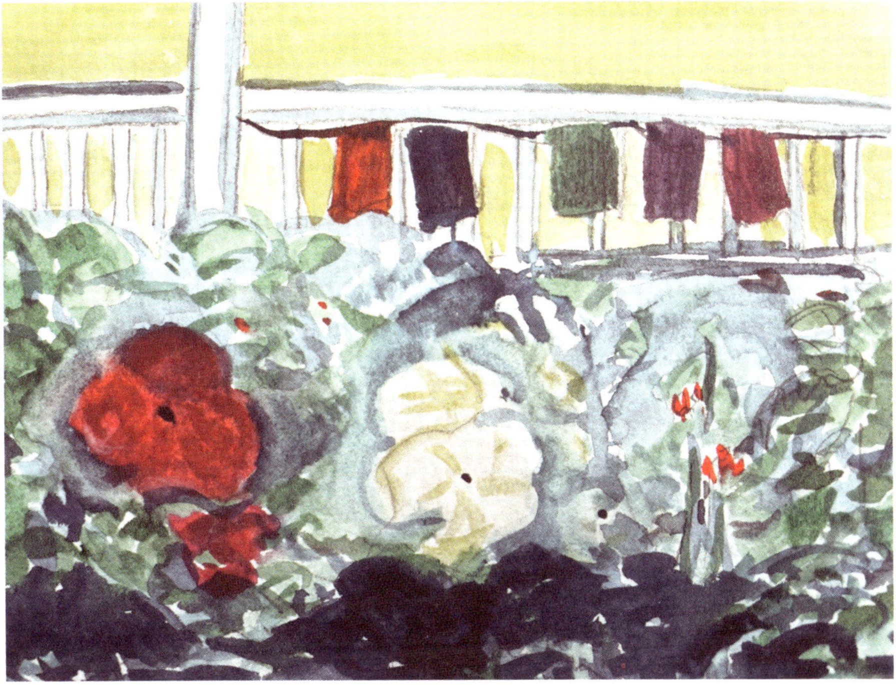

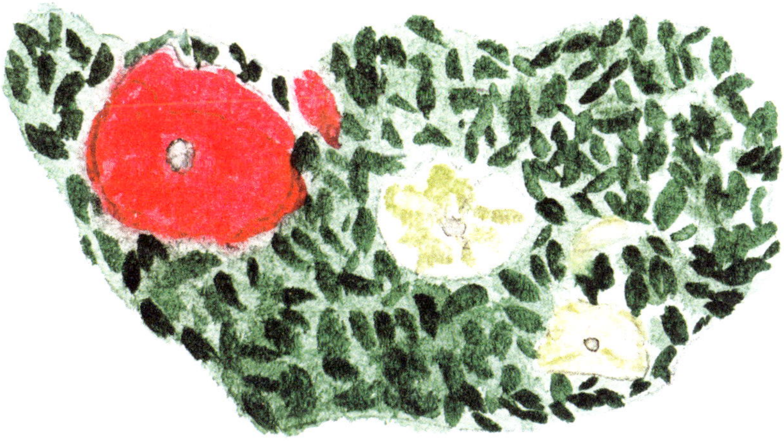

London Grey

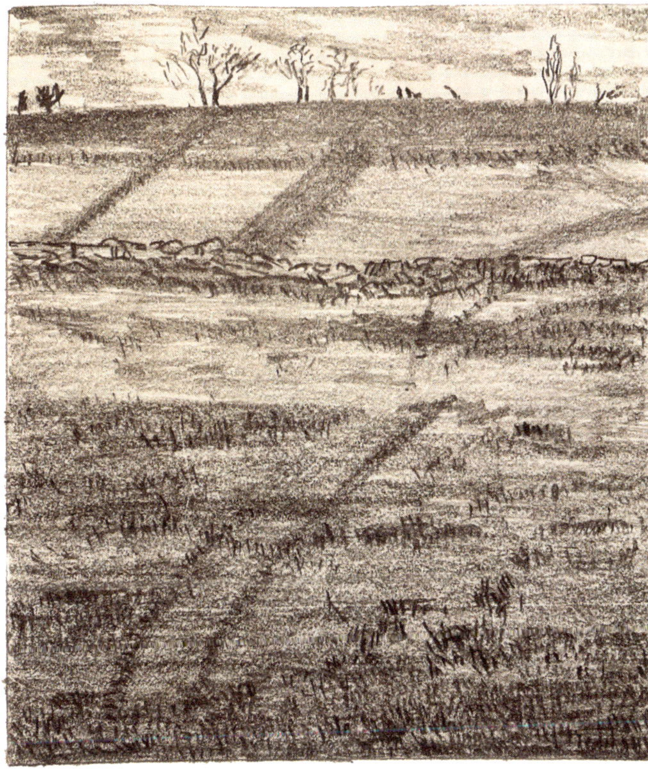

Hampstead Heath, London, 2021

See enough and write it down, I tell myself, and then some morning when the world seems drained of wonder, some day when I am only going through the motions of doing what I am supposed to do … on that bankrupt morning I will simply open my notebook and there it will all be, a forgotten account with accumulated interest, paid passage back to the world out there.
— Joan Didion

Also London itself perpetually attracts, stimulates, gives me a play & a story & a poem, without any trouble, save that of moving my legs through the streets.
— Virginia Woolf

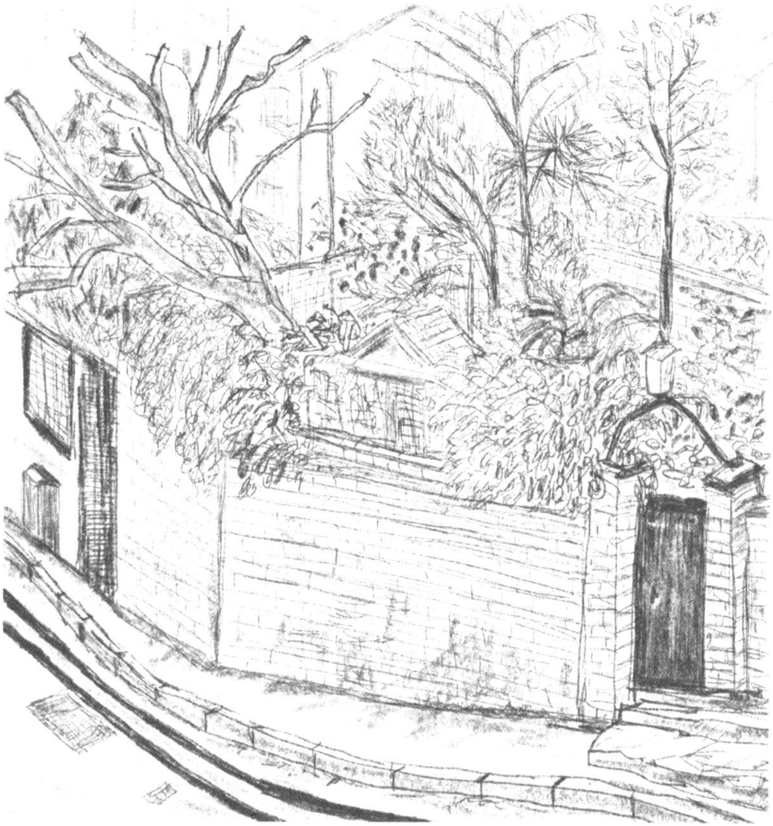

Neighbour's Garden, London, 2022

23 December 2021

Arrived in London early morning. A text from Ila saying 'Joan Didion died'. Absurd to imagine that this could mean much or change anything but I texted back that on the flight I had been listening on Audible to Didion's novel *Play It as It Lays*.

24 December 2021

5 a.m. Jet-lagged. Last night I watched again the Didion documentary *The Center Will Not Hold*. Found the exchange below in an interview and wrote it down in my notebook.

> *Interviewer*: You have said that writing is a hostile act; I have always wanted to ask you why.
> *Didion*: It's hostile in that you're trying to make somebody see something the way you see it, trying to impose your idea, your picture. It's hostile to try to wrench around someone else's mind that way. Quite often you want to tell somebody your dream, your nightmare. Well, nobody wants to hear about someone else's dream, good or bad; nobody wants to walk around with it. The writer is always tricking the reader into listening to the dream.

25 December 2021

Read an extraordinary 1998 piece by Didion on Hemingway. Emilie sent me a poem: 'Night School' by Louise Glück. The poem is about an art teacher instructing the poet, offering her hope. 'The work will come,' he says to her. 'Start small.'

News on my phone from the *Evening Standard*: 'London's Omicron crisis grows as one in 20 had Covid last week' and 'London records most Covid infections as UK tops 1.4m cases in a week'. From the *Times*: 'Omicron variant Covid rates soar in London hotspots'. My students don't arrive here until 10 January. I have no idea whether they will be allowed to come.

Before I left the US, I sent out a note to all the students who would be arriving in a fortnight. It was encouraging, I told them, that a lot of our learning was going to take place on the streets where the virus was less of a threat. My course is called 'Black London: Walking Diaries'. We will walk the routes taken by the characters in the stories we are reading and make journal entries about everything we do. The journal as a record of reading and writing. Sent a suggestion to the students: 'Keep a journal of these days and the days that will follow. Note down the news if you want, or simply what you are feeling. Or the literature you are reading. Whatever gives shape to your days and that, when noted down, will give a coherence to the life you inhabit.' Attached a little piece from the *New York Times Magazine* and this sketch I made today of berries that Mona had brought from outside Ferry House on our campus.

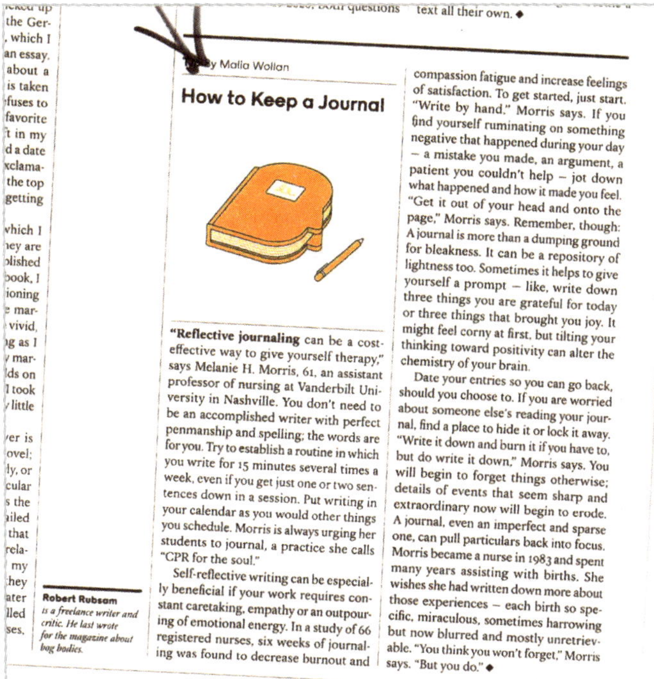

text all their own. ◆

By Malia Wollan

How to Keep a Journal

"Reflective journaling can be a cost-effective way to give yourself therapy," says Melanie H. Morris, 61, an assistant professor of nursing at Vanderbilt University in Nashville. You don't need to be an accomplished writer with perfect penmanship and spelling; the words are for you. Try to establish a routine in which you write for 15 minutes several times a week, even if you get just one or two sentences down in a session. Put writing in your calendar as you would other things you schedule. Morris is always urging her students to journal, a practice she calls "CPR for the soul."

Self-reflective writing can be especially beneficial if your work requires constant caretaking, empathy or an outpouring of emotional energy. In a study of 66 registered nurses, six weeks of journaling was found to decrease burnout and compassion fatigue and increase feelings of satisfaction. To get started, just start. "Write by hand," Morris says. If you find yourself ruminating on something negative that happened during your day – a mistake you made, an argument, a patient you couldn't help – jot down what happened and how it made you feel. "Get it out of your head and onto the page," Morris says. Remember, though: A journal is more than a dumping ground for bleakness. It can be a repository of lightness too. Sometimes it helps to give yourself a prompt – like, write down three things you are grateful for today or three things that brought you joy. It might feel corny at first, but tilting your thinking toward positivity can alter the chemistry of your brain.

Date your entries so you can go back, should you choose to. If you are worried about someone else's reading your journal, find a place to hide it or lock it away. "Write it down and burn it if you have to, but do write it down," Morris says. You will begin to forget things otherwise; details of events that seem sharp and extraordinary now will begin to erode. A journal, even an imperfect and sparse one, can pull particulars back into focus. Morris became a nurse in 1983 and spent many years assisting with births. She wishes she had written down more about those experiences – each birth so specific, miraculous, sometimes harrowing but now blurred and mostly unretrievable. "You think you won't forget," Morris says. "But you do." ◆

Robert Rubsam *is a freelance writer and critic. He last wrote for the magazine about bog bodies.*

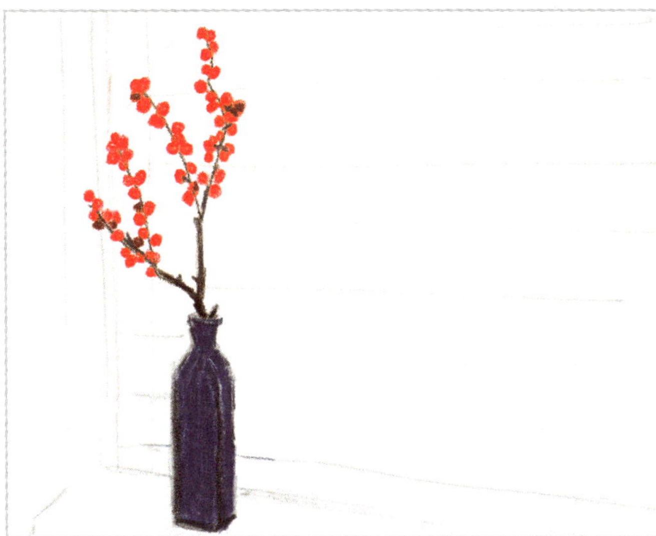

Ferry House Berries,
Poughkeepsie,
New York,
December 2021

26 December 2021

We are in a new place and there is uncertainty about what the future holds. I haven't ventured out much. But reading and drawing have given me a way to bind myself to a place and time.

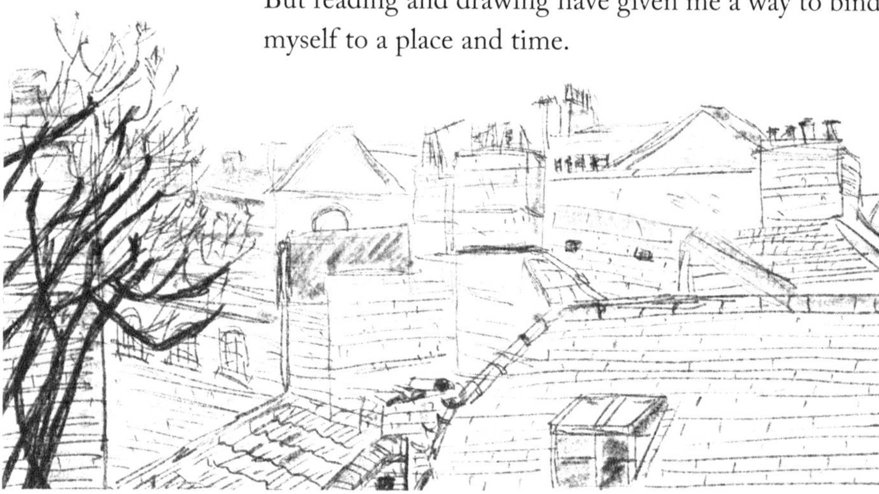

London Grey, London, 2022

Yiyun sent a note yesterday asking if there was 'any good book that would teach a complete novice how to draw flowers and plants'. I immediately wrote back that only yesterday I had started reading *Drawing on the Right Side of the Brain*. I made a note of an entry in that book where beneath several small sketches the author quotes Henning Nelms: 'In the history of inventions, many creative ideas began with small sketches. The examples above are by Galileo, Jefferson, Faraday, and Edison.' When I read those words I thought of James McPhee's demand that his students first draw a diagram to show the structure of their essays. And then that thought led to the idea that I might ask my students to draw a map of their experiences and their emotions during their time in London.

27 December 2021

Sent Yiyun an extract from *Drawing on the Right Side of the Brain*. In a letter to his brother, Theo, who had suggested that Vincent become a painter, Vincent van Gogh wrote: '… at the time when you spoke of my becoming a painter, I thought it very impractical and would not hear of it. What made me stop doubting was reading a clear book on perspective, Cassange's *Guide to the ABC of Drawing*, and a week later I drew the interior of a kitchen with stove, chair, table and window—in their places and on their legs—whereas before it had seemed to me that getting depth and the right perspective into a drawing was witchcraft or pure chance.' Yiyun's reply came: 'OHHH!'

28 December 2021

Rahul and I went to the street on which his school is located in Chalk Farm. My first time on the Tube during this trip. Came back and didn't venture out again. At night, spoke to my former student Favor who wanted to interview me on the subject of migration. In response to what I was saying about having left India, he offered me an aphorism from his native Hausa: 'Kowa ya bar gida, gida ya bar shi.' (Whoever leaves the home, the home leaves him.)

Earlier, Ravish posted a picture on Instagram, of some writing on a wall: 'Mahesh and Annu, Hasampur, 10 March 2005.' Ravish had questions.

> Does Mahesh still love Annu in 2021? Did Annu know of his love? Did the two meet here together on 10 March 2005 and declare their love? What did the March breeze feel like that day? There would have been the yearning of Holi or maybe spring had arrived carrying the sound of summer's approaching footsteps? The two people whose names appear on this wall have completed a journey of sixteen more years. Do the signs of love last longer on walls or in our memories? Is there a writer or a poet who can answer these questions? Is there anyone out there?

When I saw Ravish's post, nearly forty thousand people had liked it. I did too. In my mind I was thinking that there is a book here. Go to Hasampur. Ask for Mahesh and Annu. Even if one was unable to find Mahesh and Annu, one would still find many other Mahesh and Annus.

30 December 2021

In response to a note from Teju, I said that I had mostly been only to Hampstead Heath for long walks. And to the grocery store nearby. (My phone showed that my steps were 'trending higher for 5 days: 10, 699'.) Teju wrote back: 'Be super super cautious with the virus. The level of contagion beggars belief.' Also:

'Send notes. I love to receive news of the decline of the British Empire.'

Rahul and I went on a trip in the city on bus number 24. Hampstead Heath to Pimlico, past Westminster Abbey and Trafalgar Square. On the Embankment, there was a monument to the dead in the Second World War. On the plinth, a quote from Churchill: 'Never was so much owed by so many to so few.' Rahul posed in front of the monument with his palms open, asking the question, 'Where are the Indians?'

31 December 2021

I hadn't walked on this section of the Heath. Took pictures and made a drawing of the stretch of grass in my new notebook.

Outside all the restaurants in Hampstead Village, delivery men standing beside their scooters or motorbikes. These men wear heavy, protective clothing, almost always black, and they have big round helmets on their heads which they seldom take off. If, instead of this journal, I were writing a short story set in London, it would probably be about a South Asian man—Nepali? Sri Lankan?—who is a delivery guy on a motorcycle. It is night, the road is wet after the rains, he is racing to make a delivery, keeping up an incessant honking on his vehicle. He makes a steep turn … But that is not the real problem. His troubles start when he arrives at a door. The woman accepting the delivery asks him to remove his mask. Not comprehending, he does. She asks him to turn around and show his face to the CCTV camera …

2 January 2022

Picked up a newspaper left on the Tube. 'Pupils told to wear masks in classrooms'. Rahul's meeting at the school has been moved from 4 January to a week later. Instead of starting classes, the school will be vaccinating students and staff during the first week of the new term.

Most of my sketches have been made while looking out of the kitchen window that faces the church. Today I stood at the other kitchen window that overlooks the neighbour's house and I drew the middle-aged woman who comes out regularly on her balcony to smoke. My sketch of the woman bent over her chair, smoking, wasn't any good. I'll make a good drawing of her before we leave London! That is my new year's resolution.

3 January 2022

On the Tube today, an idea came to me: I'll make a map of the titles of the books I see being read by my co-passengers.

Went to the Tate Modern to see what I could share with my students and I found the perfect exhibit for the class. 'The British Library' by Yinka Shonibare CBE. The installation has 2,700 titles and printed in gold on the spines of these books are the names of first- or second-generation immigrants to Britain. Many of them are writers whose names I recognized (including names that we will read in our class) but there are also others whose near-anonymous contributions to British life are acknowledged here. The books are bound in Dutch wax-print fabric, which I learnt from the display, is a material with a complex relationship to colonialism. Developed in the Netherlands as a mass-produced imitation of Indonesian batik—when Indonesia was a Dutch colony—it found a market in west and central Africa where it was adopted and absorbed into local traditions. There was an invitation at the exhibit for visitors to submit their stories or their responses. I hope my students will want to contribute to this archive.

7 January 2022

Suddenly remembered it is the anniversary of my mother's death today.

I only make small drawings. They are usually completed in a single sitting. On occasion, I have to wait for the paint to dry before I can make additions. But gouache dries quickly and my wait is never longer than a few minutes. For the first time in a long time, I made a small painting that took me three days to

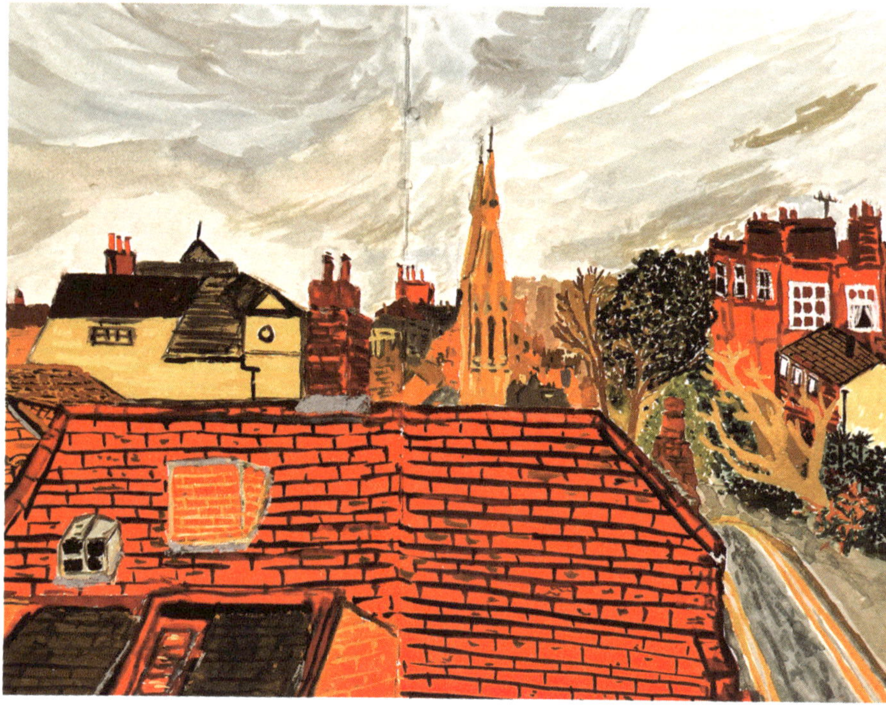

Outside My Kitchen Window, London, 2022

complete. It is a view of Hampstead, the view outside the kitchen window. This flat doesn't have a desk, so I use the kitchen island to do my work. I look at this scene every day for several hours. For the two weeks I have been here, I have often looked at the gloomy skies outside and made drawings. But then, the other day when the sun came out after the rain, everything looked bright and full of colour. I began the painting then, not thinking that it would take as long as it did. I posted the image on Instagram with the caption: 'Riding the fine line between fiction and non-fiction, a view of what I can see outside my kitchen window here in London. Gouache on paper.'

9 January 2022

It is Sunday today. The ringing of church bells. Then the whoosh of a vacuum cleaner in our flat. I had written two days ago to Hanif Kureishi to tell him about the course I was going to teach. Could he go for a walk with us? I told him he would be paid a small honorarium. I haven't seen Hanif for longer than a decade, it seems. We were last together at the 2010 Jaipur Literature Festival. When our conversation on the stage was over and the audience was allowed to ask questions, a man took the microphone. He wanted to know if Hanif was circumcised. Despite being taken aback, Hanif said, 'Jesus, it's been a long time since anyone has shown any interest in my genitalia.'

Hanif's reply to my request regarding class came today. He also asked if I was here with the family and how long I would be staying. After I sent my response, he wrote back, 'Ah, so good, Amitava—keep a diary.' I'm filing this in the Universe-Sends-Me-A-Sign Department.

Also, after many failed attempts at sketching her, here's a painting I made today of the smoker in the house across from us. Ritual fascinates me. Consider my innumerable disquisitions on writing every day, a modest goal of one hundred and fifty words; and walking every day, mindful walking for at least ten minutes. Or making the check mark in your journal. My London neighbour is of interest to me because she follows a simple, uncomplicated ritual of smoking every two hours. She comes out on her tiny balcony, her glasses pushed high on her head, and after lighting up, leans heavily on the chair to finish her smoke. After a few minutes, she returns inside. Writers steal other people's lives to put into their stories. I want to imagine she is working on a wonderful project and I wish this stranger, whom I have sketched half a dozen times, all the luck in the world.

10 January 2022

My students arrived from New York. I was there on Goldsmiths campus a bit before 9 a.m. to wait for the bus bringing them from Heathrow. Their plane had arrived on time around 7.30 a.m. But there were delays. From a nearby Sainsbury's I got sandwiches and drinks for them. I'm glad I did because when the bus brought them to Loring Hall they were glassy-eyed with exhaustion. They collected their keys and Covid test-kits and then their food from me. In two days, we have plans to meet at Trafalgar Square for a walk on the Strand.

11 January 2022

The Blue Book comes out next month and the publishers in India want some language about it. The copy I wrote this morning starts with the Picasso quote about painting being just another way of keeping a diary and ends with my assertion

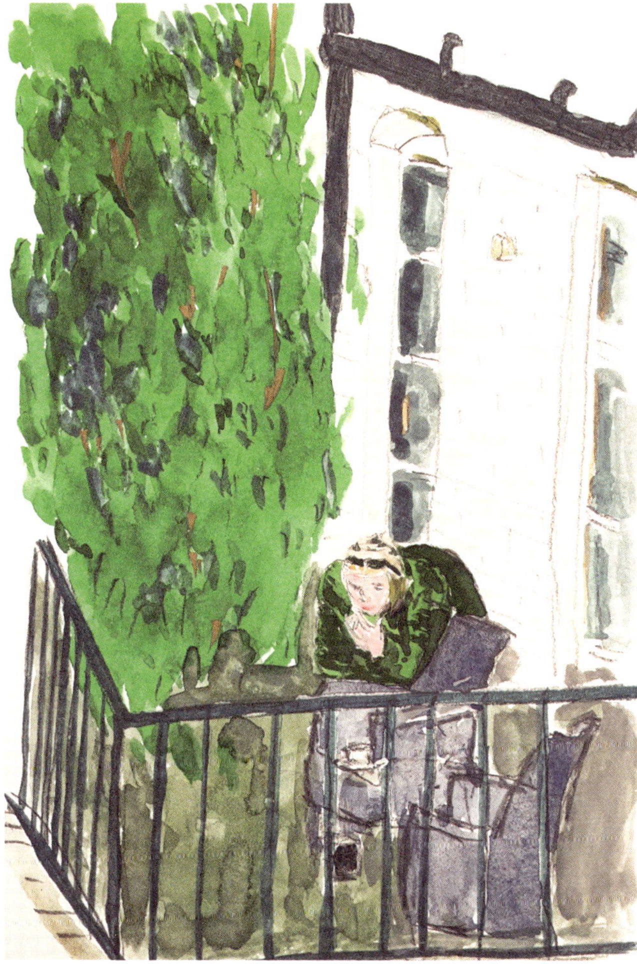

Smoker on Balcony, London, 2022

that beauty exists only if you notice it. I believe in this more strongly perhaps because I'm deep in my middle age: don't let your life pass unnoticed. Now, a question arises: what will I write as copy for *The Yellow Book*? Here is my first attempt: 'One day passes. Then another. A whole succession of days turning into months and years. How to mark our separate days? The places we have been. Our individual passions, our pain. Against the blurring of years, the clarity of a record. And even amidst crises, how to keep creativity alive?' I want these books to be read for the way in which memory is distilled in their pages.

In the afternoon, had my first conversation with my new editor at Knopf, Diana Miller. We had a pleasant Zoom chat. She has read the draft of my novel *My Beloved Life*. The novel has two main sections: an account of an older man's life that begins with his death from Covid, and the story of his daughter's life. Diana likes the book but without being pushy she raised questions about structure. How will the reader know that the daughter's account will come later? Can we introduce her story earlier and more substantially? Also, the mention of Covid so early makes the story too much about the contemporary moment. Perhaps hold it off for later? I'm giving myself a month for making daily revisions.

12 January 2022

At the reception desk at Goldsmiths, the woman was giving me instructions on how to use the Covid test. Explaining the final step, she said, 'You won't have experience of this, but it is like a pregnancy test. You'll see a sign on the stick.' And I sang out, 'But I do, I do. I remember those days of tension and excitement.' Then I turned around to point at Ila standing behind me near the pillar. 'And this child was the result.' The lady, laughing now, clapped loudly and so did the woman seated next to her.

I collected my students and we made our way to Trafalgar Square. The idea was to follow the route taken by Virginia Woolf on the Strand as she looks to buy a pencil ('an excuse for walking half across London between tea and dinner'). The text as a map. That is what I wanted my students to grasp. As a map for walking, yes, but also a map for writing brief essays. Were the students interested in what I was saying as we walked? I don't know. It is too early to know.

We headed to Chinatown for a late lunch. Earlier, at Trafalgar Square, I had noticed a young Indian couple, heavily made up, feeding pigeons. There was a sign nearby asking people not to do this. After lunch, we ran into the couple again near Piccadilly Circus. The young woman in a flagrant pink coat and her partner with a shadow of a beard that was almost certainly only make-up. I found out now, amidst cameras and reflectors, that they were the leads in a Bhojpuri film. When I started speaking in Bhojpuri to them, the film-maker, a polite middle-aged man with his moustache dyed black, urged me to stay. But I ran away to where my students were waiting.

हम सोचनी कि हमार मेहरारू घरे हमार बाट जोहत होखीहन। हम बस ना ना करके बैल हांकत घरे चल देनी। (It occurred to me that my wife must be waiting for my return. I just said, no, no, and driving my bullocks hard, I headed for home.)

15 January 2022

Took students to the Tate Modern. Term at Goldsmiths doesn't start till next week (and there is talk of an impending strike) but I had read in a previous director's report that students feel lost during this week when they are waiting. Better to engage them in activities. I took them first to the Yinka Shonibare CBE exhibit. Then the Media Networks Rooms because there are ideas there about what they can do with their independent projects. (Rokni Haerizadeh, an Iranian-born artist, paints over media images from television of protests in his native Tehran. Wilhelm Sansal, a Polish artist, paints images from what is circulated in the media. Example: an oil painting of Gaddafi's corpse. Or the installation by Cildo Meireles with hundreds of radios, each tuned to a different station, the whole assemblage built in the shape of a tower to evoke Babel.) Within five minutes a student was outside checking his phone. Was he finished, I asked and he said he had to deal with insurance issues. That was a sign. A little later another student said she had to return to the dorm; she was unwell. We went to the Lubaina Himid exhibit. At one point, I gathered the students around to talk a bit about what themes of the Black diaspora and life in London were reflected in a particular work of Himid's. A few blank faces and I wondered if tiredness from jet lag and the problems that day because of the Tube strike had led to this lack of enthusiasm. Pearl, the programme assistant, texted to ask about the trip. 'Low energy,' I replied.

17 January 2022

Wrote to the students this morning that it was their first actual day of the term and they must adopt a daily ritual. A new practice, specific to London. Take a walk, or make a clipping from the free newspaper outside the Tube station, note down what you see outside your window, go for a run, take a picture of the first coffee of the day—any particular ritual whose record will vividly evoke for you, and for anyone else, a sense of what it meant for you to have spent thirteen or fourteen weeks in London. Told them about a colleague at Vassar who wakes up and notes down the weather. He now has a record going back decades. I decided I was going to make a drawing every day.

Ila left for Heathrow at 7.45. Rahul said he wanted to talk to his grandfather. I called my father in Patna but he appeared a bit lost and unwilling to talk. Wrote a note about this to my sisters and Dibu said that he has been sleeping a lot. She sent a picture she had taken for me. His eyes sunken, mouth dark, hair short and dishevelled. A death mask.

Took Rahul to the Heath to kick around a soccer ball. The field was soggy. Extracted the iPad from the backpack and made a sketch of the Golders Hill Girl sculpture. It is a brass sculpture of a young woman in shorts and a tee; she is sitting on the ground, her leg crossed. A pair of brass flip-flops rest near her. Charming and dull. My drawing of the sculpture was, of course, much worse than the bad sculpture itself.

Rahul Holding Mask on Hampstead Heath, London, 2022

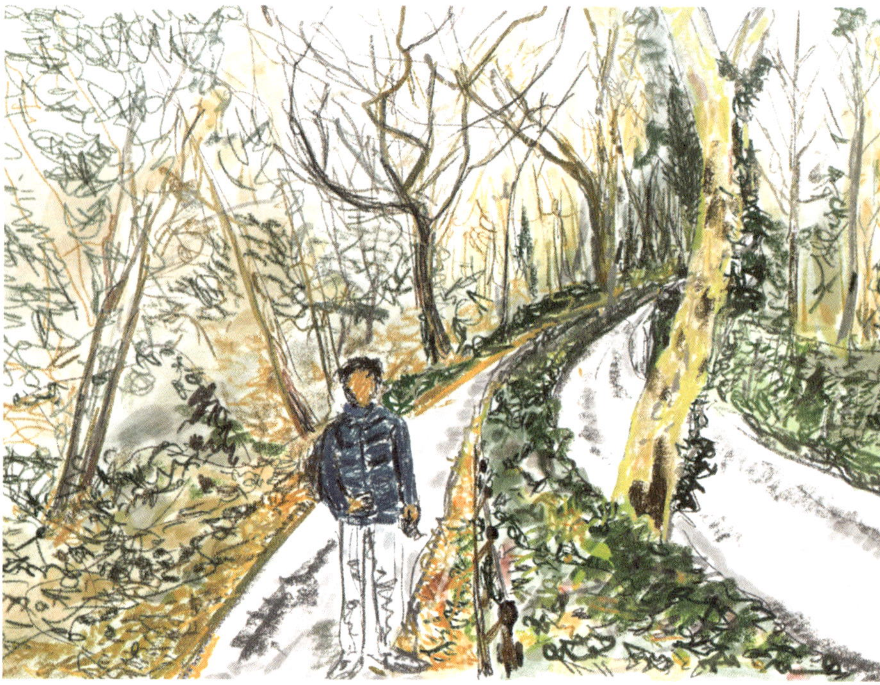

18 January 2022

Yesterday I asked Dibu if Papa is still able to recite dates and numbers like he has done all his life. I panicked when I sensed his disorientation on the phone yesterday. Could we be seeing signs of approaching dementia? I always suspect I'm getting Alzheimer's when I can't recall names of my students

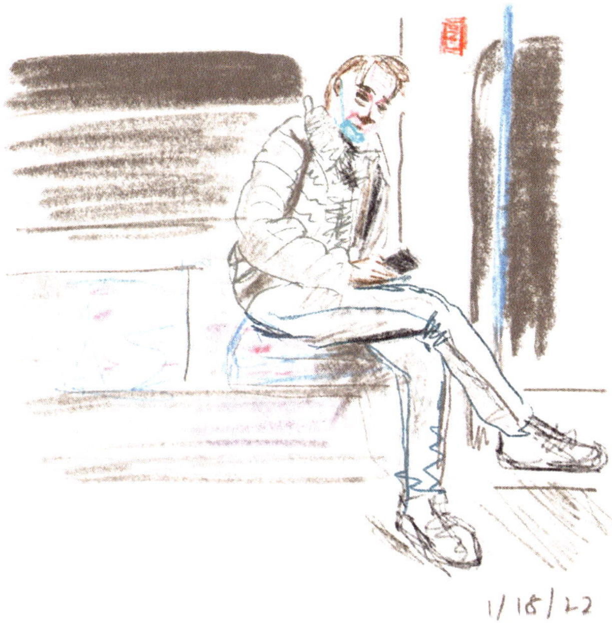

My Name Is Omicron, London, 2022

or colleagues. Dibu wrote back to say that today was the first time Papa got out of bed to sit on a chair and read. He lists dates and figures in his characteristic way but she doesn't know if they are accurate. He has no social interaction. I had sent my note on WhatsApp to both my sisters. After Dibu, it was Didi who responded. She said that Papa was unable to recall the bank account number the other day. He is usually able to rattle off all such numbers without difficulty and this had caused her to stop and worry. I can see that my use of the word dementia has sent her mind spinning into the void.

(Made the sketch on the previous page in the train after dropping off Rahul for his first day of school. The improperly worn mask sets my teeth on edge.)

19 January 2022

Titles seen on the Tube so far, mostly on the Northern Line: *Adults in the Room* by Yanis Varoufakis; *The Gita*; *Confucian Analects* by Ezra Pound; *Swing Time* by Zadie Smith; *Porno* by Irvine Welsh; and, on the Jubilee Line, a baby in her stroller with a book in her hand, the words saying: 'Hooray. At last. A Blue Bicycle Rode Past'. If someone else was doing what I am doing, they would note in their diary that they had seen a man reading *The Lonely Londoners* by Sam Selvon.

21 January 2022

Found out that Chiki Sarkar's sweet little boy has died from drowning during a holiday in Sri Lanka. There is no easy way to confirm the details of this news; I don't want to ask anyone. I've met Chiki three or four times, including once in her home, maybe six years ago, when she was pregnant with this child. Chiki had founded her new publishing house a year or two earlier and we had a discussion about what I was writing. But this news … A darkness has descended over me. Mona asked if I had written to Chiki. I said no. What could I possibly write?

Dear Chiki, Nothing that I can say, or anyone can say, will take away the unbearable pain of this loss. I send you all my love and condolences. I hold your hand and offer my inadequate sympathy and support in the face of this sorrow beyond everything.

22 January 2022

Hampstead Grove, London, 2022

Next week, my class is meeting Hanif Kureishi. In preparation for the visit, I read Zadie Smith's essay

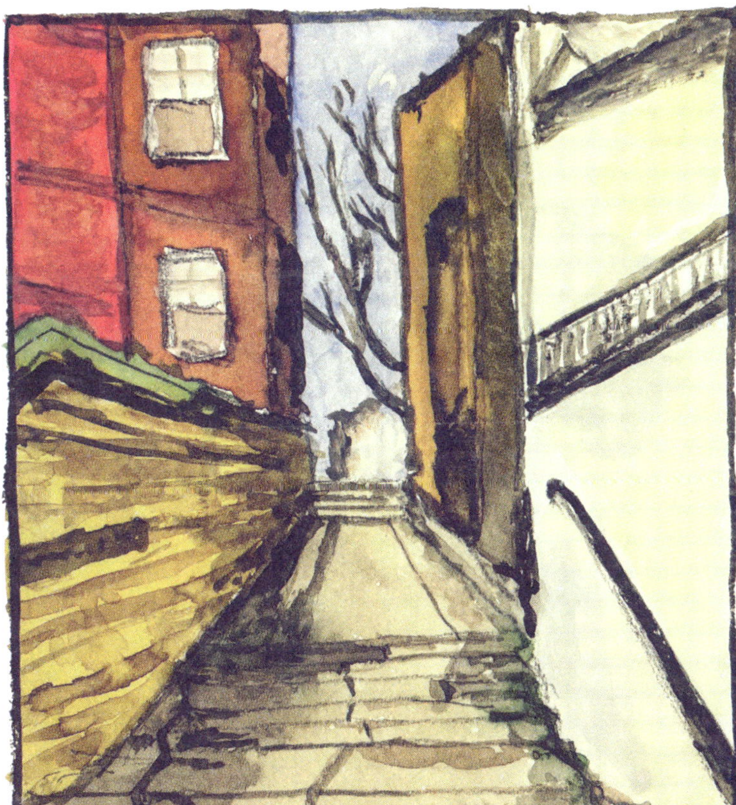

on *The Buddha of Suburbia*. So smart that essay, in so many ways. My favourite line:

> From the point of view of our 21st-century world, where the only possible reaction to anything seems to be outraged offence, I find it a relief to go back to more innocent days and remember a time when we were not all such delicate flowers that every man's casual idiocy had the awesome power to offend us to our very cores.

Kureishi's Karim mocks the ignorance and bigotry of others but he is also amused by them. That is what Smith is celebrating in this line. But the reason why my mind fastened on to the phrase about 'outraged offence' is because of something that happened in my class last week. We screened an episode of Steve McQueen's *Small Axe*. This was the Mangrove episode about the police violence in Notting Hill that resulted in the trial of the Mangrove Nine at Old Bailey in 1970. Before I got home that night, there were two complaints on my phone from students: I should have issued a trigger warning; there wasn't any debriefing, etc. The truth was that Pearl hadn't used the words 'trigger warning', but she had told them exactly what the film portrayed. We had run out of time because the person from the Goldsmith's study abroad programme had come to make an announcement and that took nearly half an hour. The students were right to point out that there hadn't been time to discuss the film. Valid point but no generosity at all about the thought behind our choice of materials for class. Or that we would discuss the film during the following class. I was perhaps overreacting when I remarked to Mona that I hoped the students were putting as much effort into their journal entries as they were into their long judgemental missives which had politeness on the surface but violence at their heart. My turn for having a go at outraged offence.

23 January 2022

Every once in a while someone will put up this quote by Cicero on social media. It is so good that I haven't checked to see if it is accurate. This is what the meme says: *Times are bad. Children no longer obey their parents and everyone is writing a book. — Cicero, 43 BCE*

24 January 2022

I was making a little drawing of our street when the doorbell rang. The mailman had brought two advance copies of *The Blue Book*. Mona, a busy woman, writing her own book on the imperialism of finance, hasn't read my books (I'm not complaining) but she took a copy in hand and immediately declared it the most beautiful thing I have done (I'm bragging). Sent a PDF to my agent in New York to see if it can be published in the West. And all my gratitude to Hemali Sodhi and Udayan Mitra.

Am listening on Audible to Sally Rooney's *Beautiful World, Where Are You*. Her protagonist comments acerbically on writers who 'pretend to be obsessed with death and grief and fascism—when really they're obsessed with whether their latest book will get reviewed in the *New York Times*'. That is so very good! I have told myself many times over the past few weeks and months, while reading reviews of *A Time Outside This Time*, that the only way for me to have distance from negative reviews, some of which I regard as illiterate or in bad faith, is to also not get too excited or happy about positive reviews. More importantly, focus on finding new forms to accurately express observations on death and grief and fascism.

The Mount, London, 2022

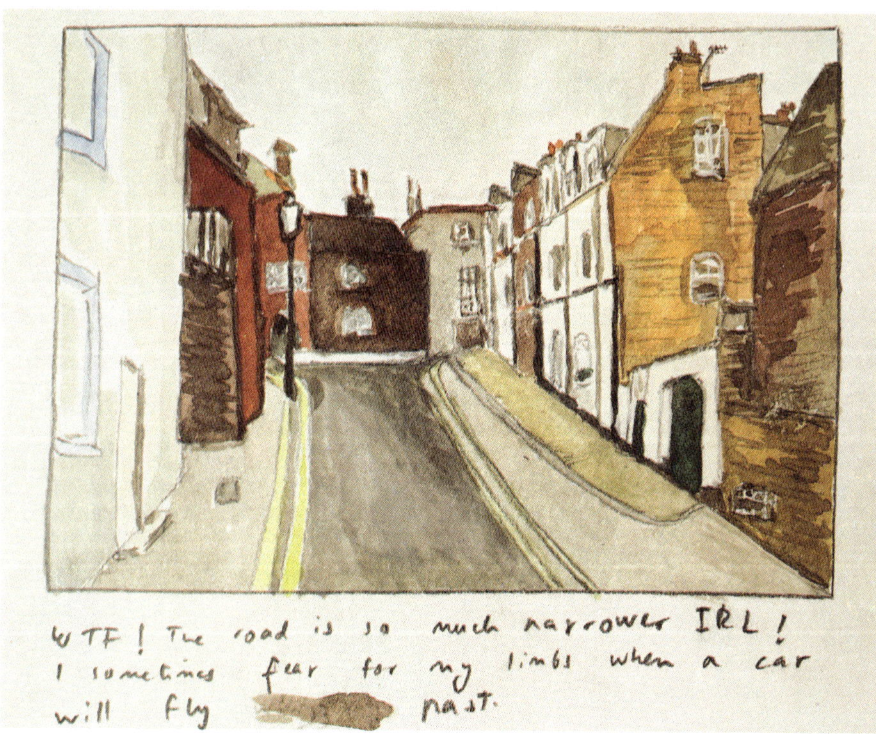

25 January 2022

A poet friend told his students that they couldn't be real writers if they were unable to name the trees around them. What are these trees that I see in London? I believe this process of pruning is called pollarding.

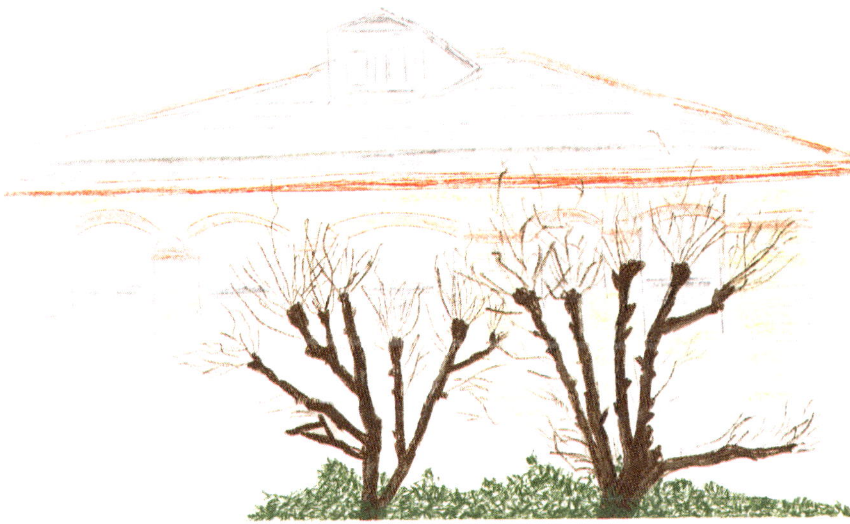

Trees on Kemplay Road, London, 2022

Went for a walk with Mona on Kemplay Road. At night, watched *The Art of Looking* on BBC Channel 4 about John Berger. John Christie had told me on the phone about it. Put the show on pause to note down what Jean Mohr was saying about Berger not liking the overly aesthetic photos that Mohr produced during their collaboration. 'He was wary of photos that are too beautiful. He liked those that looked almost accidental.'

To produce writing and paintings that are not too precious. Isn't that my goal?

26 January 2022

We met with Hanif Kureishi in a café in Shepherd's Bush. He is still his old self, sharp, funny, provocative. I asked him to give advice to my students about keeping a journal while we were in London. Hanif said, 'When I get up in the morning, I go to my desk and do some free writing. Free writing means that you just write down any crap that occurs to you. I usually write down things that I saw yesterday, somebody said something funny, somebody said something moving, I suddenly saw something on the street, an argument or a dispute, something I read in the newspaper, something that is going on politically. I look back at this material and find lines, bits of dialogue, funny things that I can integrate into my writing. The point of keeping a diary is not to torture you with another pointless discipline; the point of keeping a diary is to have a kind of a record of material that you may or may not use later. For me, it is just a way to keep writing, to keep your hand moving, to keep working. And you will notice things then during the day because you know you might note them down. And I always carry a notebook with me, I've got it in my bag, I write down stuff that interests me. I'm a writer. It's my job. Sometimes I take photographs. Everyone has a camera now. I take pictures of something I just see on the street. It is noticing really what things attract you, actually, what turns you on. It's usually where your libido is. What are you looking at, why are you looking at that colour, why are you looking at that person. It's libidinous, it deals with excitement, what interests you about the world, what turns you on about the world. It's just to focus you really.'

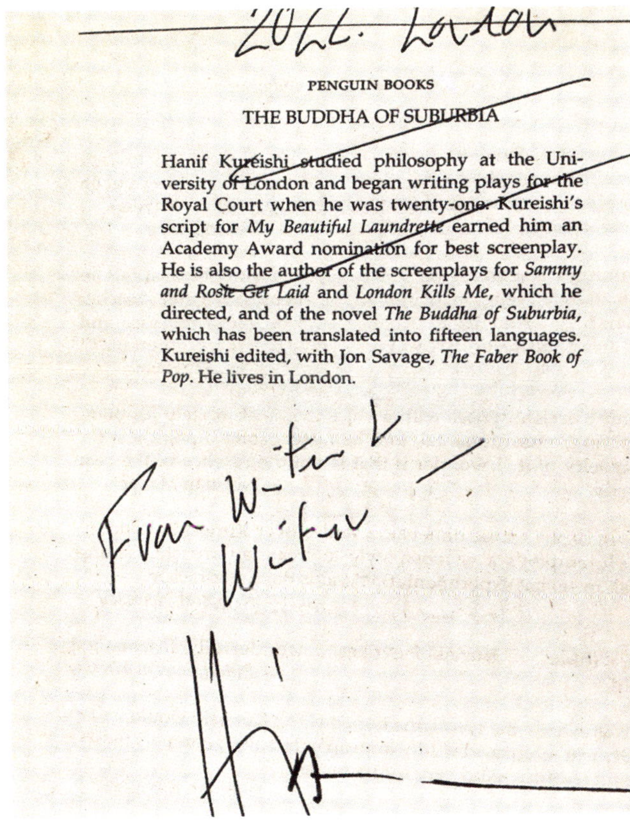

PENGUIN BOOKS

THE BUDDHA OF SUBURBIA

Hanif Kureishi studied philosophy at the University of London and began writing plays for the Royal Court when he was twenty-one. Kureishi's script for *My Beautiful Laundrette* earned him an Academy Award nomination for best screenplay. He is also the author of the screenplays for *Sammy and Rosie Get Laid* and *London Kills Me*, which he directed, and of the novel *The Buddha of Suburbia*, which has been translated into fifteen languages. Kureishi edited, with Jon Savage, *The Faber Book of Pop*. He lives in London.

From Writer to Writer, London, 2022

When Hanif was about to leave, I asked him to sign my copy of *The Buddha of Suburbia*. Then the students and I talked about the rest of the course; they were worried about the structure of the course and wanted me to pin down in exact detail our meetings in the future. But it has been difficult to organize visits with the different writers. I would like us to be open to improvisation. Still, I told them that I had a precise idea of the following month and emailed those details when I came home. On the train I was thinking that thirty years have passed since I first read *The Buddha of Suburbia*, a wonderful and exuberant novel about leaving behind not just the suburbs and all that is old, but also about how to find newness through a curiosity about art, about music and sex. The voice I adopted in *Immigrant, Montana* owes a lot to Kureishi's Karim. My narrator even quotes him. I've known Hanif now for twenty years but it struck me today that when I first read him I had, of course, wanted to be a writer, but could scarcely have dared imagine an inscription like the one above. It's a long road. Maybe that is what I should've told my students at the end of class today.

Drawing of Door
with NYPL Tote,
London, 2022

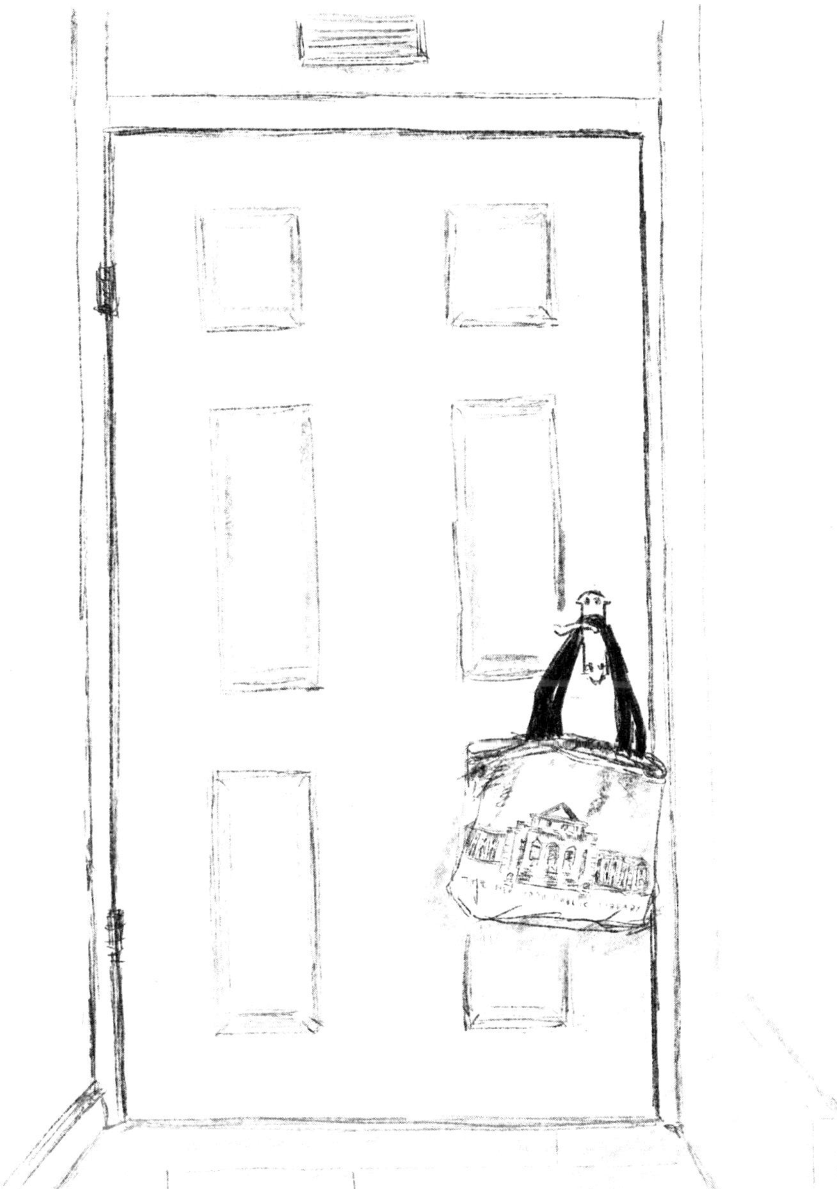

27 January 2022

For the past fortnight, I have been giving some time every day to the draft of my novel. For the most part, small changes to the beginning and the end. Then, I came across this quote from Anne Enright in my notebook. What had made me photocopy it in the first place, and that too in large font? I can't remember. Yesterday, I sent it as an email attachment to Diana Miller at Knopf, telling her that my ten-weeks-to-live self was quite happy with the revisions I was making in my draft. Diana wrote back today: 'That is a tall order from Anne Enright.' The trick, I think, is to try to live a very long life and, simultaneously, keep reminding oneself that time is running out.

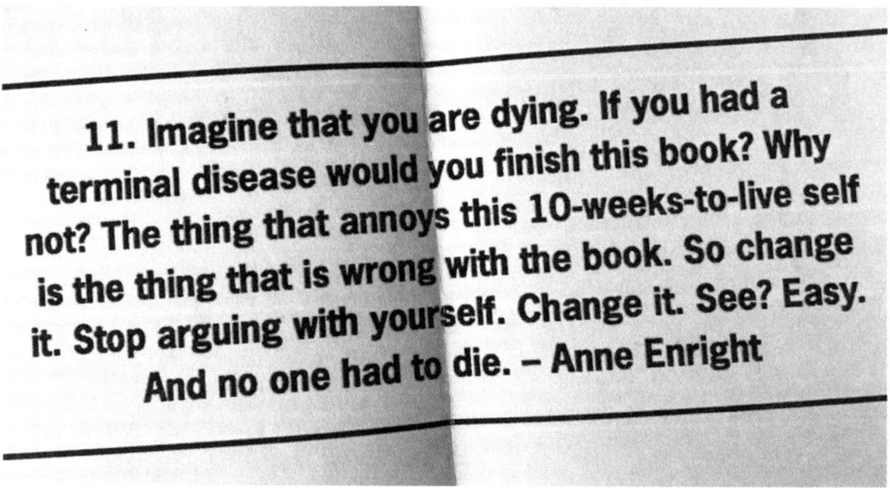
11. Imagine that you are dying. If you had a terminal disease would you finish this book? Why not? The thing that annoys this 10-weeks-to-live self is the thing that is wrong with the book. So change it. Stop arguing with yourself. Change it. See? Easy. And no one had to die. – Anne Enright

In the evening, I spoke over Zoom to the students at Ryerson University in Toronto who are reading *Every*

Day I Write the Book. A lot of questions about my rules of writing, healthy habits, Covid, patience and failure. The class that the students are enrolled in is called 'Creativity, Writing and Everyday Life'. I told them that I had never had the good fortune during my decades of education of being taught a course on the everyday. But all education must, must, must be linked to the everyday, particularly in the liberal arts.

Came across an artwork on Instagram via Sotheby's. David Shrigley, b. 1968. Linoleum cut, 2018. Large block letters on a black background. 'My Artwork Is Terrible and I Am a Very Bad Person.'

28 January 2022

I usually work in the kitchen but the rental agency said that they needed to show the flat to prospective tenants. Carrying a photocopy of an out-of-print book, *The Third Reich of Dreams*, I went down to a coffee shop in Hampstead Village. The book I was reading was the work of Charlotte Beradt who, after Hitler came to power, began to secretly record the dreams of her fellow Germans. I loved Beradt's description of the dreams as 'diaries of the night'. I had found this book several months ago as I contemplated the idea of collecting dreams during the pandemic; then, I realized I had been more or less sleeping because one day, only a month after I told my agent that I wanted to work on a project on dreams, I saw in the *New York Times Magazine* an article about a Harvard psychiatrist named Deirdre Barrett who had been collecting dreams about Covid from the very beginning of the pandemic. In the café in Hampstead Village, as I read more pages from *The Third Reich of Dreams*, I thought of Freud whose statue I had seen during a walk back to my flat from the grocery store Waitrose on Finchley Road. I knew that Freud's last home was also somewhere close to the statue. For a change, the sun was shining outside. Twenty minutes later, I was outside an elegant Victorian home at 20, Maresfield Gardens. Two blue plaques on the wall outside, one for Freud and one for his daughter.

20, Maresfield Gardens, London, 2022

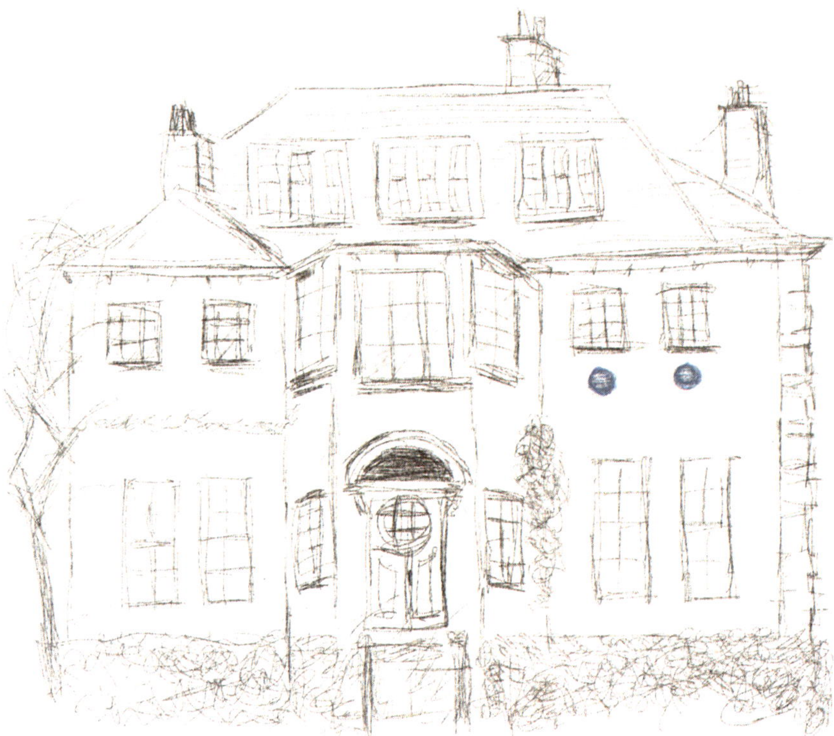

29 January 2022

Weekend. Woke up at 5 a.m. and wrote two hundred words in my draft and then went back to sleep. Woke up at 10 a.m. and made a watercolour that I didn't like much.

I was thinking of what a student told me earlier this week. She had a different expectation when she came to London—that her dorm would be an old building in an academic setting. Instead, she came to Loring Hall off a scruffy and crowded street near the New Cross Gate station. It struck me later that these students grew up with Harry Potter when they were children. They want Hogwarts.

30 January 2022

Anniversary of Gandhi's assassination. There were several paintings put up on Instagram. The one that caught my eye was by Krishen Khanna: a tight cluster of people, each reading a newspaper, the blank white of the newspaper open like a shroud. '*News of Gandhiji's Death*, 1948.'

31 January 2022

I was sitting with Mona after dinner and asked her what she would like for her birthday. Actually, I said, 'What would you like for breakfast, what would you like for lunch, what would you like for dinner?' Rahul was doing his homework on the couch. He looked up and said, 'I don't want to kill the vibe but I just need to share the information with you that the man who had betrayed Anne Frank was identified after seventy-seven years.'

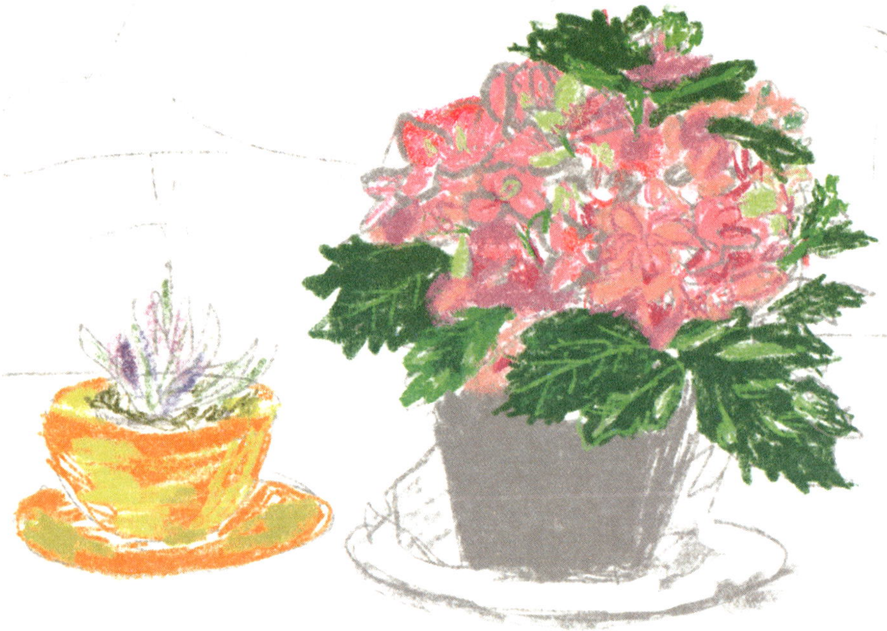

Flowers for Mona, London, 2022

1 February 2022

Today, a third student tested positive. 'Not feeling great, but fine overall.' I cancelled class for Wednesday saying that we will meet over Zoom instead. If they are in quarantine, I want them to watch films that would belong in our course: *My Son the Fanatic*; *Dirty Pretty Things*; *Brick Lane*; *Bhaji on the Beach*; *East Is East*. Bought plants and a candle for Mona.

2 February 2022

Woke up to several notifications on my Twitter feed. Pritish Nandy had tweeted to his nearly two million followers about *The Blue Book*: 'This must be one of the most fascinating books I have read in recent times.' What could I say? I went on social media and wrote about what I owed him and had learnt from him so long ago: 'Arre sirji, what do you know! All those years ago when a boy read *The Illustrated Weekly of India* that you edited … Thank you.'

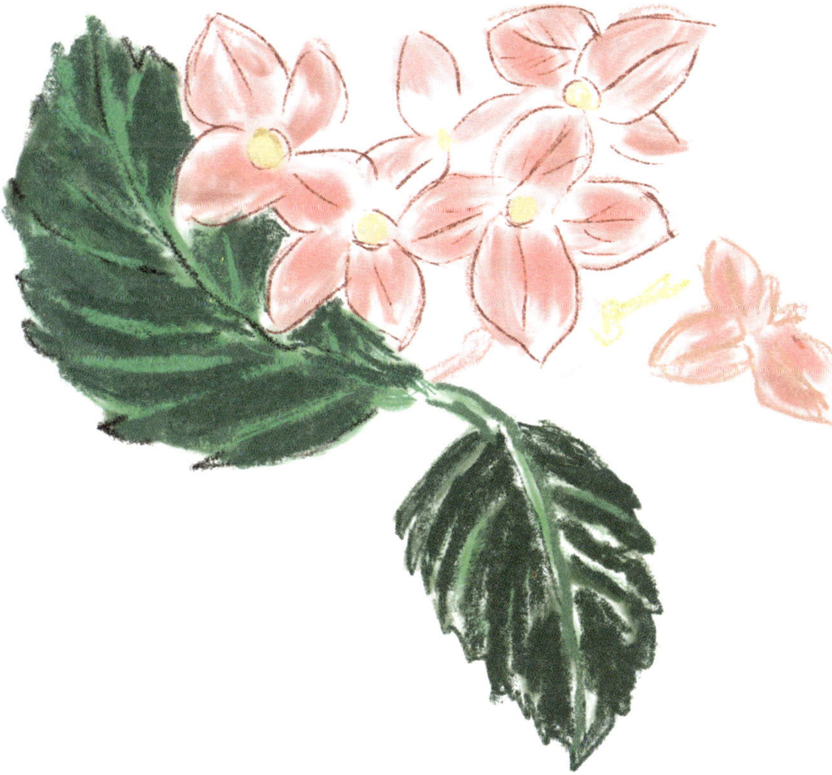

Flowers for Mona, London, 2022

Yellow Sun

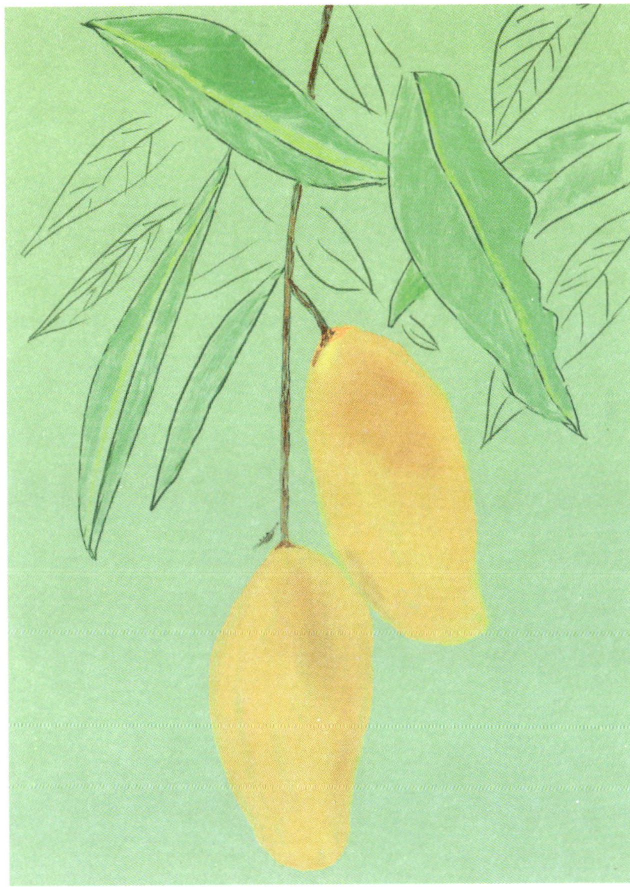

Dreaming of Mangoes, London, 2022

3 February 2022

First Zoom class in London, and it went very badly. Was on Goldsmiths campus but my laptop couldn't access their Wi-Fi. Rushed to the computer support office and they said that my laptop, given to me by Vassar, was encrypted in such a manner that they couldn't help me. Went to a nearby Costa and paid for coffee before getting the password. I was late; class had started fifteen minutes earlier. Pearl was discussing elements of free writing. But the Costa Wi-Fi didn't work either. Bought an hour of internet connectivity from BT wireless. This time I was able to connect. The class was discussing—what exactly? It was loud in Costa and now that I had Wi-Fi I told the students that I would join them in five minutes. Ran across the street and up the stairs of the building where I have an office. When I opened my laptop there, I saw that the campus had a firewall. I couldn't go back to my BT connection. For the first time I was prepared to honour the rule in the UK that you are allowed to drink if you are eighteen. I offered to buy a round of drinks at a nearby pub for all my students. Only one showed up; she was generous and carried back lattes for the students in quarantine.

4 February 2022

I had seen a sign above an Indian off-licence and painted it. When I posted it on social media, the writer Zia Haider Rahman commented that the store was on Drummond Street. He explained that he had Googled the telephone number on my drawing. I told him that I had been hoping that someone would do that. I told him that all art is fiction, of course, but I like the frisson of the real. He agreed with the sentiment. (Many years ago, when reading Jonathan Safran Foer's *Extremely Loud and Incredibly Close*, I came across a phone number. I don't have the book here with me in London. Whose number was it? In any case, I remember that I called the number in the novel and the phone rang for a really long time. What was I going to say if someone had answered it? *Hello, is that Jonathan?*)

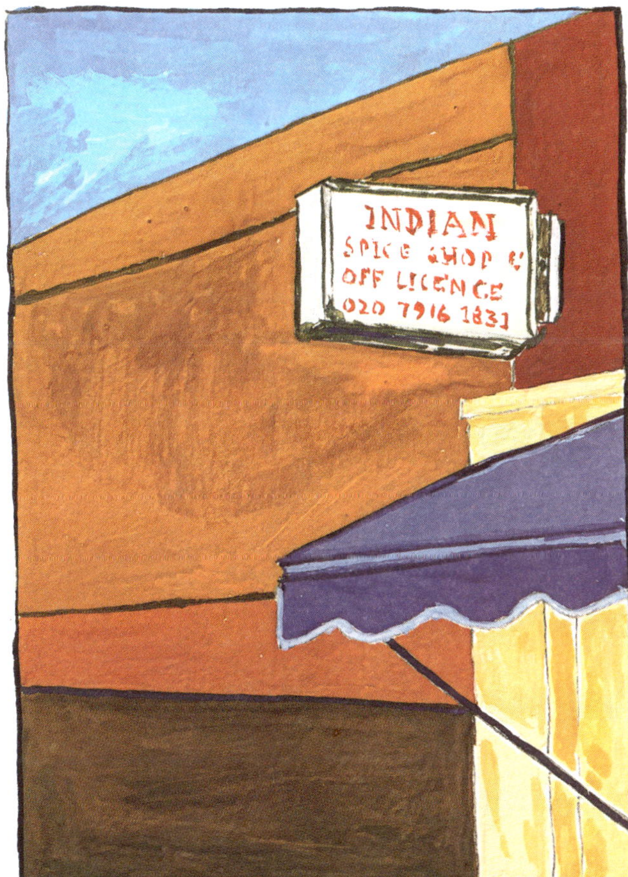

Drummond Street, London, 2022

5 February 2022

Bitterly cold day. Met Ian Jack at the Angel Station and we walked along the Regents Canal. We were among a lot of tourists. Ian said that when he marvelled at the thousands of young foreigners there on the canal tow path, his son had said that those people were in 'the pursuit of authenticity'. Every guidebook to every city has a section about leaving the tourist trail and going somewhere else. The Canal walk was it. There were boats moored all along the Canal. One had a sign: 'The Enemy Doesn't Arrive By Boat. He Arrives By Limousine.' People were out walking, jogging and even kayaking. I saw the locks being opened by a pretty young woman. She cheerfully

Walk with Ian, London, 2022

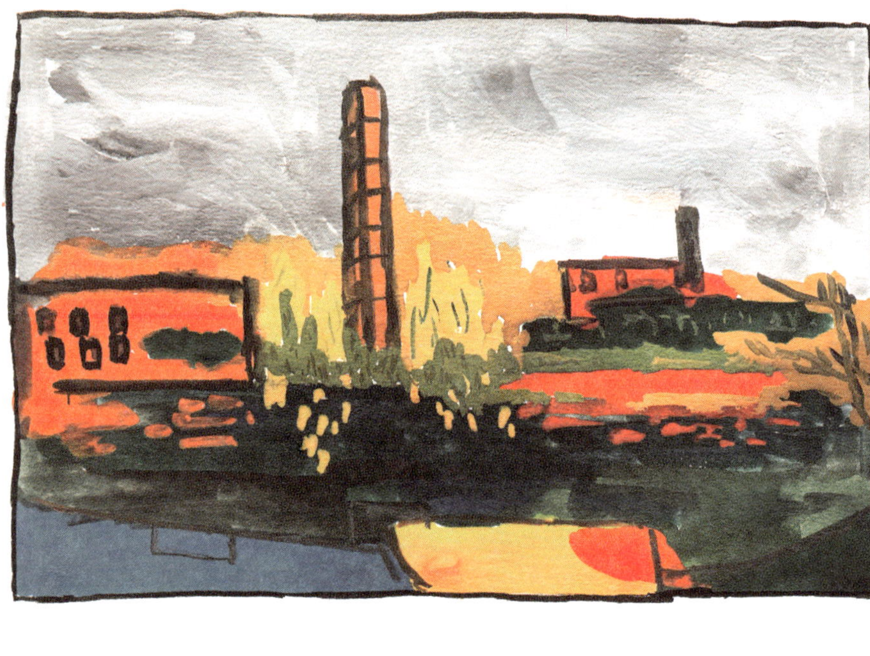

explained that she was doing this so that her friend's boat could pass downstream. I told Ian about the fights over water in Bihar. Someone upstream would make a cut in the canal and steal the water. People were armed and blood was shed over water needed for the crops.

7 February 2022

Went to Goldsmiths to show solidarity at the picket line. About a hundred people protesting. A banner waving at the entrance: 'Picket Line Do Not Cross'. Also a small dog wearing a sign #GOLDSTRIKE. I talked to a few of the professors assembled there. Apart from protesting poor pay and pension cuts, the people at Goldsmiths are particularly concerned about the way the administration proposes to lop off courses in History and English and Creative Writing. The senior management has made no concessions on any of the demands. There was coffee and tea being served from a table at the front. A group of men and women in their late sixties or seventies went up and sang some songs that must have been sung at protests for decades. There was something both familiar and tired about the event. Or almost. I didn't understand the banner that said 'Goldsmiths Is Pre-Occupied' although I understood that it was a joke.

8 February 2022

Kamila Shamsie took our class for a walk past the Grand Union Canal. In her novel *Home Fire*, Eamonn Lone walks that route, leaving behind the posh environs of Holland Park and moving past scenes of industrial blight towards the mixed neighbourhood near Preston Road. 'Always these other Londons in London,' he thinks. I asked Kamila whether it was a 'postcolonial gesture' on her part to rewrite the story of *Antigone* by using British Muslim characters in present-day London. She said no. There was a fresco on display in the Lahore Museum which showed a scene from *Antigone*. She was there in Pakistan in 200 BCE. In that sense, her appearance in the novel was more of a homecoming. I forgot to ask Kamila if the much-praised closing scene of the novel owed anything to the Bollywood thriller *Dil Se*, starring Shah Rukh Khan and Manisha Koirala.

Later, the students wanted to know if they would be allowed to travel. I said there were rules forbidding travel but I couldn't advise them not to get on a train and go somewhere close or far. Wasn't that what study abroad was also supposed to represent? My only condition was that I didn't want anyone to travel alone. They had to take care of each other. We worked out an awkward compromise. I wouldn't be told if they were leaving the country but they would inform Pearl. I said that I didn't want to lose my job and my reputation if they did something stupid. And please, please, please always tell your parents what you are doing.

Before I went to the meeting, I completed a painting from a photograph I had taken of Kenwood House during a walk on the Heath about a week ago. I had

Nadal–Medvedev, 2–2 before the Final Set, London, 2022

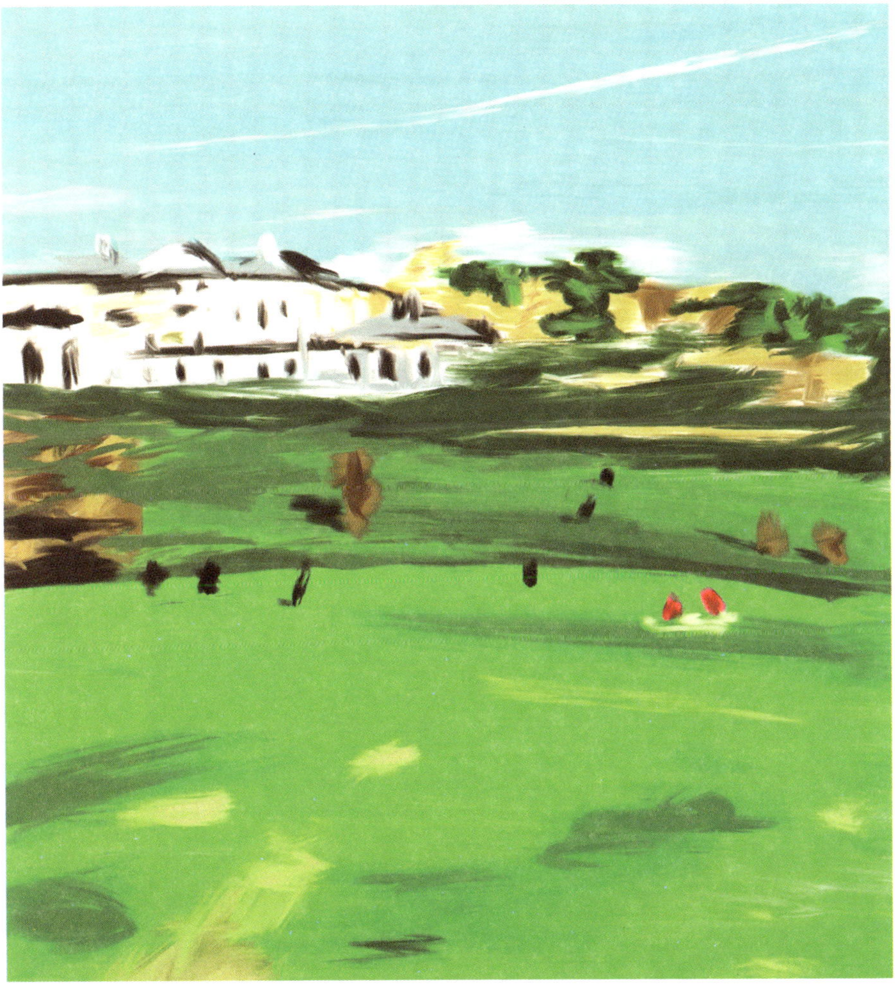

gone out that day because there was no TV coverage here of the Australian Open; I could only follow the tennis match on radio or by checking the score online. I would refresh my phone over and over during the walk.

9 February 2022

Got a message from Zadie about *The Blue Book*. 'i meant to read a page of it late last night and instead i read the whole thing and then suffered on the school run this morning. a lovely thing …' Those words, all in lower case, thrilled me. Still full of the excitement that those words had brought me, I wrote back to her saying that Teju and I have this constant back-and-forth about what he or others are going to read at my funeral. We joke about my angry letters to a former dean at my college or a writer we both thought quite obnoxious. I said to Zadie that now I'll have to leave instructions about this recent message from her. Teju might want her to just tape it on her phone and send it so that it can be played before the music starts. There was a hyperlink to Henryk Górecki's Symphony no. 3 with Dawn Upshaw as the soprano. Zadie, sweet Zadie, wrote back immediately: 'my phone cannot record anything ... i'll just have to come in person.'

10 February 2022

Today I made a drawing in the morning pages—and then, out of love, also added colour—of the plant I had

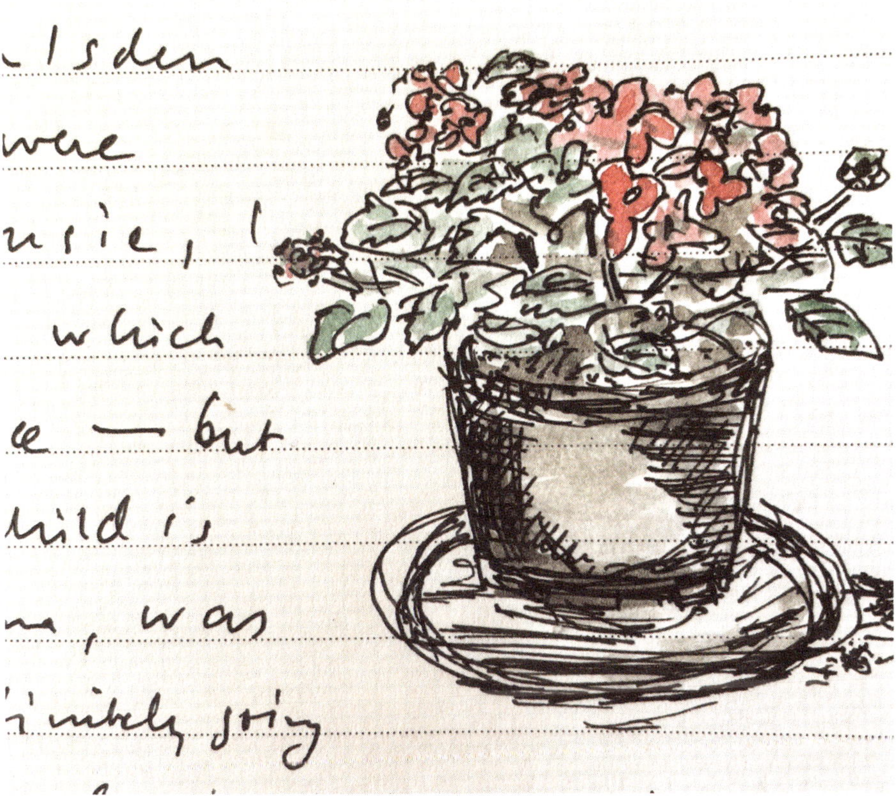

Morning Pages, London, 2022

bought for Mona. We had to rescue it after the wind knocked it down into the neighbour's yard and we could get it back only after the weekend. I drew it to give it yet another life.

Last night I started reading a piece in the *Atlantic* on friendship. Jennifer Senior writes that the key is for friends 'to make contact a priority'. I sent the link for the article to a few friends, adding a brief note about how much I valued their presence in my life.

I like the blue-and-white sign on the trains saying 'Air on Our Tubes and Trains Is Refreshed Every 3 Minutes'. My map of reading, again mostly on the Northern Line, has introduced me to a few titles I have read but also others that I had never heard of: *Say Nothing* by Patrick Radden Keefe; *Surface Detail* by Iain Banks; *The Poppy War* by R.F. Kuang; and, just today, on the overground back from Goldsmiths, *59 Seconds* by Richard Wiseman.

11 February 2022

My father's birthday. Rahul left him a message on WhatsApp and Didi recorded his reply. I met Claire Messud's friend Shefali who said that her parents had aged twenty years during the pandemic. The social isolation had taken a terrible toll. We were walking in Regent's Park. It struck me that instead of dementia what might have happened to my father was closer to depression. I have decided that I will go and visit him as soon as my work here in London is over. This means I will be in Patna in late April or early May.

12 February 2022

I had gone to sleep after looking at pictures Didi had sent from Patna. She had arranged for a puja at home for Papa. I looked at the priest in the photos that Didi had posted and entertained the macabre thought that this same man would officiate at my father's cremation. It wasn't surprising that I woke up this

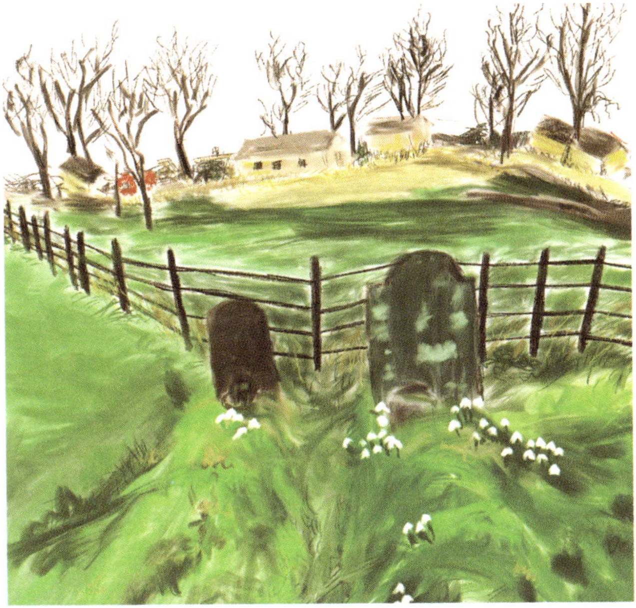

In the Middle of February, Oxfordshire, 2022

morning from a dream about my father. I was saying goodbye. I remember wondering in my dream if he would be alive when I visited him next time.

14 February 2022

We have come to the Cotswolds in Oxfordshire for three days while Rahul's school is on a break. The cottage we have rented abuts a church and a graveyard and beyond that are green fields. I find it all extraordinarily beautiful. The most striking thing about these rolling fields are these small wooden posts driven into the ground: the posts have white badges and yellow arrows and the words Public Footpath printed on them. A friend sent a link to an article in the *Guardian* from which I learnt that back in 1801 commissioners were appointed to designate rights of way in the process of enclosing common land. The article reports on an 'undeclared war' between landowners and walkers. It ends by saying that 'many Britons have a nostalgia for the fields and moors of the imagination. It is a part of the national identity, as the writer Robert MacFarlane powerfully argues.' I got interested in this phenomenon of the public pathways because of the course I'm teaching. We are walking in the city and what this outing has reminded me of is

In the Middle of February, Oxfordshire, 2022

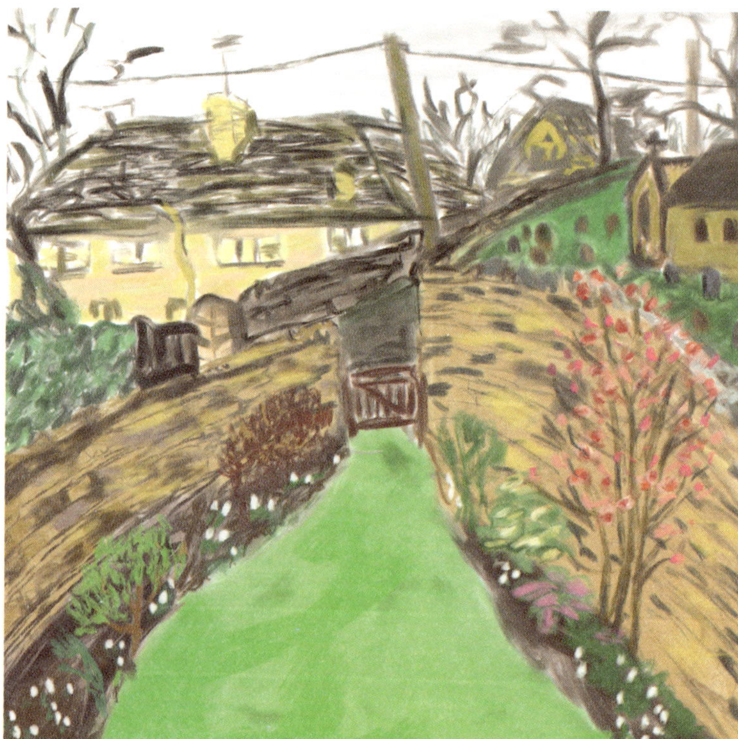

that there is a different relationship with the land and, indeed, with citizenship, to be explored by going on rambles in the rural parts.

15 February 2022

A quick trip in the evening to hear journalist Barkha Dutt talking about Narendra Modi at Oxford University. She told the audience that the Bharatiya Janata Party's propaganda was a kind of psy-ops. An Indian woman in the audience asked what she could do as a citizen and Barkha said that everyone could stop watching bad or compromised media and, instead, try to support independent voices. What you

Heath Street, London, 2022

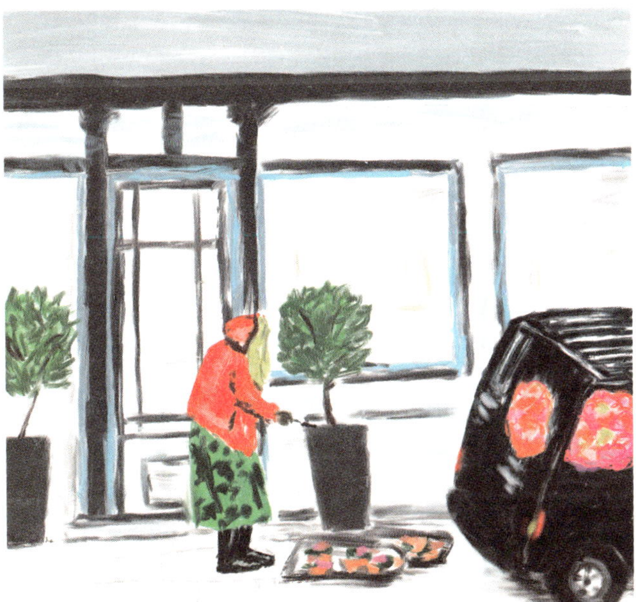

spend on one Starbucks coffee you could give to these alternative media sources each month.

Later, we agreed that we could support independent media by taking Barkha out for dinner when she returns to London.

16 February 2022

Took students to the National Gallery to watch Kehinde Wiley's short film *Prelude* for which he put Black Londoners in the snowy wastes of Norway. About half a dozen Black people of different ages in colourful garb surrounded by a snowy solitude. A series of striking visuals, with a sense of stillness at the heart, but I was left a bit uncertain about the metaphorical meaning that lurked nearby, something beyond an impression of an encounter with nature. Even a confrontation perhaps, between the human and the non-human, between Black people and the vastness of the natural world. We were also supposed to have read a batch of poems, mostly by Caribbean poets in London. In the foyer of the museum, I spoke a bit about the poems to the students but from their faces I could tell that there wasn't any interest in what I was saying. We then went to the British Library so that we could look at the display of Andrea Levy's manuscripts. In another month, we are going to watch the adaptation of Levy's *Small Island* at the National Theatre.

17 February 2022

A board with writing in chalk outside the pub closest to our flat: 'Cloudy … with a chance of beer.'

18 February 2022

Snowdrops have appeared in flowerbeds. And crocuses. A storm named Eunice sent fierce winds across the island. There were government warnings to stay indoors. The doors and windows in this flat making an insistent, wind-pressed noise. The tops of trees tossing like someone violently shaking their heads. On the nearby church steeple that is being repaired, white polythene fluttering in the breeze.

Wind on the Heath, London, 2022

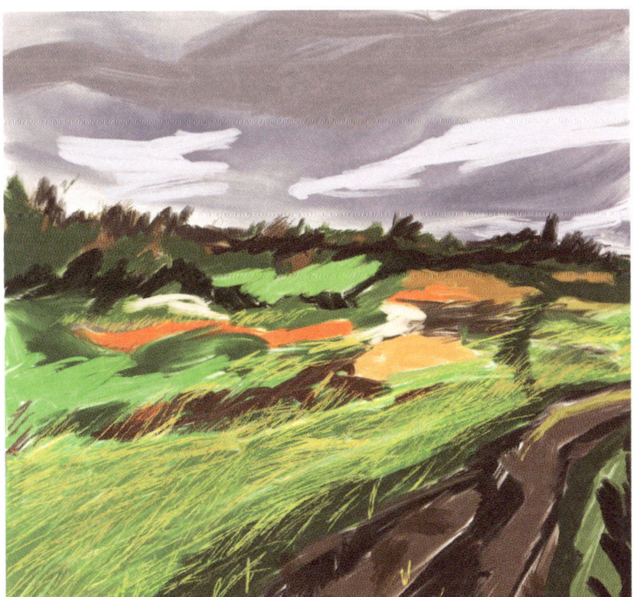

Now and then a leaf will race across the window. But no, that wasn't a leaf, it was a pigeon. Unable to make any headway in the strong wind, it turned away swiftly after a struggle.

19 February 2022

BBC reports that three people died from the toppled trees and flying debris in the storm yesterday.

20 February 2022

Was invited to a biryani lunch. The cook was from Lucknow. She said that men were interested in her but she was saving to open her own restaurant. Went to get groceries from a nearby M&S and on the way on Belsize Road I passed a crab-apple tree. There was a slight drizzle falling, and the afternoon was chilly, but here was a sign of spring.

23 February 2022

It is 'reading week' at Goldsmiths. No classes. Students are going to places like Berlin, Edinburgh and Paris. Am reading the novel *Territory of Light* by Japanese writer Yuko Tsushima. Not having to teach today, I went to Ealing to visit the Punjabi poet Amarjit Chandan. I had seen him in the Berger documentary last month and today I got a copy of his poem about his village.

24 February 2022

Russia invaded Ukraine. A tweet quoted Eleanor Roosevelt: 'No one won the last war, and no one will win the next war.' I searched for it online and found that she had written these words in a letter to Harry Truman on 22 March 1948.

25 February 2022

Read today that a Ukrainian woman offered sunflower seeds to a Russian soldier. She wanted him to keep

Ukraine Flag, London, 2022

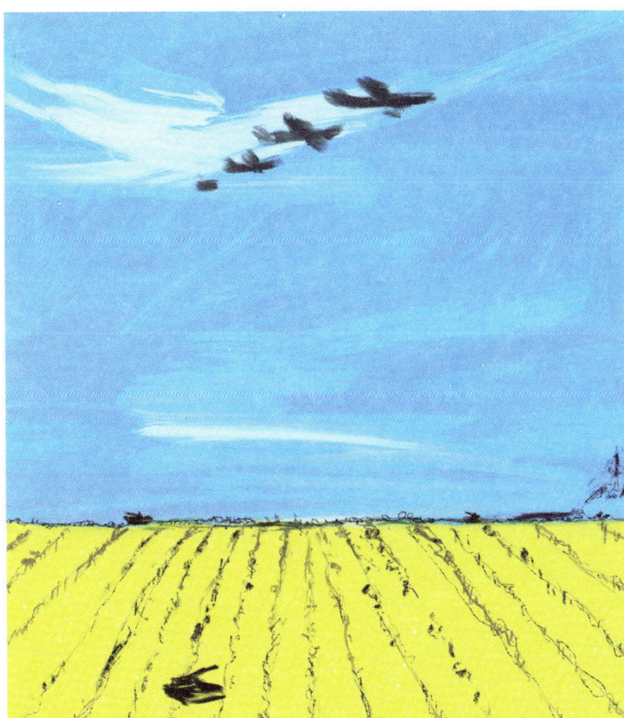

the seeds in his pocket so that when the invader was killed, sunflowers would grow where he died.

26 February 2022

Over the past three days I have been interviewed by journalists about *The Blue Book*. Today's recording was for the Jaipur Literature Festival, a conversation with Ravish Kumar. We spoke mostly in Hindi, and sometimes Bhojpuri, and I wondered whether that restricted our viewership. There are more readers in Hindi but maybe they don't download such interviews. Later, I did a series of drawings which are part of a set of proposals for a Partition Museum. I was asked to make a drawing or two: the curator wanted me think about small monuments, the whimsical, even the absurd. My small proposal involves the giving of gifts which come in pairs; the catch is that each item in the pair comes from a separate side of the border. So, for example, tea from India and sugar from Pakistan. I made cartoon-like drawings to illustrate these ideas, my thoughts no doubt also drawing upon the sense that Ukraine and Russia have a shared history.

In the last drawing, I have quoted Ali Sardar Jafri's hymn to harmony:

Tum aao gulshan-e-Lahore se chaman bardosh
Hum aayen subh-e-Banaras ki roshnee lekar

Himalaya ki havaaon ki taazgee lekar
Aur isske baad yeh poochein ki kaun dushman hai.

(You come from the garden of Lahore laden
with flowers,
We will come bearing the light of a Benares
morning
With fresh breezes from Himalayan heights
And then, together we can ask, who is the enemy.)

Small Proposal,
London, 2022

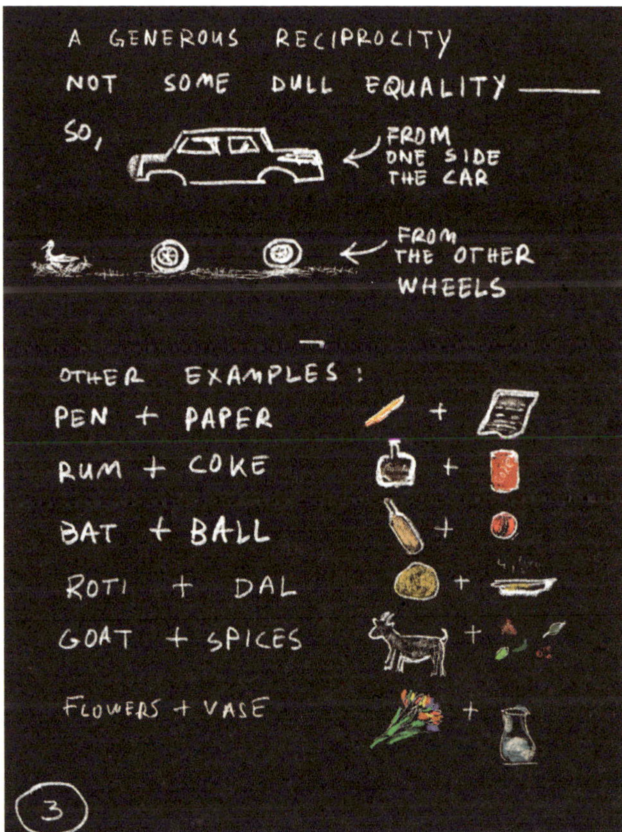

27 February 2022

I had been told that on the last Sunday of each month, a walking book club meets at Daunt Books and then goes wandering on the Heath. I had gone to the bookstore and picked up a copy of the book being read this month, Yuko Tsushima's *Territory of Light*. There was a report on it some years ago on BBC Radio 4 and, whether because of that or not, there were nearly forty people gathered today. The sun was out; a perfect day for a walk.

The organizer's name is Emily Rhodes. I was interested in what Rhodes did because here was a model for what I do every day as a teacher. You choose a book and you devise a way to engage with it imaginatively by taking your students on an adventure. The walking book club resembles what I'm doing with my walking diaries class here in London. Reading from index cards, Rhodes would offer a prompt: 'You might think that nothing much happens in this book but there are moments that stand out. Was there one moment that stood out for you?' And then we would walk for a few minutes till we arrived at a spot she had marked. We would stand around and have a brief discussion before setting out again, preferably with new partners.

At one stop, near a pond, dogs ran into the water and then ran out with their coats dripping. A woman came close to our group shouting for her dog. '*Lola!*

Lola!' When we reached the top of Parliament Hill, people around us were flying kites while others sat on benches or milled about. Tsushima's novel is about a single mother who is raising a daughter by herself in Tokyo. In a *Chicago Tribune* piece, Tsushima had said that her theme in all her work was 'love and solitude'. She had also written, 'I think children are a heavy burden for divorced women.' Our group was made up mostly of women and there was a good deal of sympathy for Tsushima's protagonist but also a good deal of criticism. Two young women who talked to me said they felt the first-person narrator remained a mystery and psychologically distant. Then I spoke to another woman, a retired lawyer, and she told me that Tsushima's father, a famous novelist in Japan, had committed suicide. Tsushima had been only an infant at that time and, no doubt, pain and incomprehension were perhaps a part of the author's own interior landscape.

At the last stop, Rhodes handed out Japanese snacks, rice crispies and seaweed. A number of the readers admitted that they had dropped their negative view about the novel's protagonist. A tall white-haired woman with colourful glass-frames said, 'When you are alone with a child, it can be bloody awful.'

28 February 2022

I made a drawing about an episode I mention in *My Beloved Life*. I'm still waiting for edits from Diana

Miller; when I spoke to her last, she had said that she liked this section about James Baldwin. Posted the drawing with the following note: 'When Baldwin was in high school, the teacher asked the boys in the classroom to step up to the blackboard and describe a scene from nature. Baldwin chose a winter scene and wrote on the board about "the houses in their little white overcoats".'

The poet Ilya Kaminsky posted a tweet yesterday in which he said that he asked an older friend in Odessa

Homage to Baldwin, London, 2022

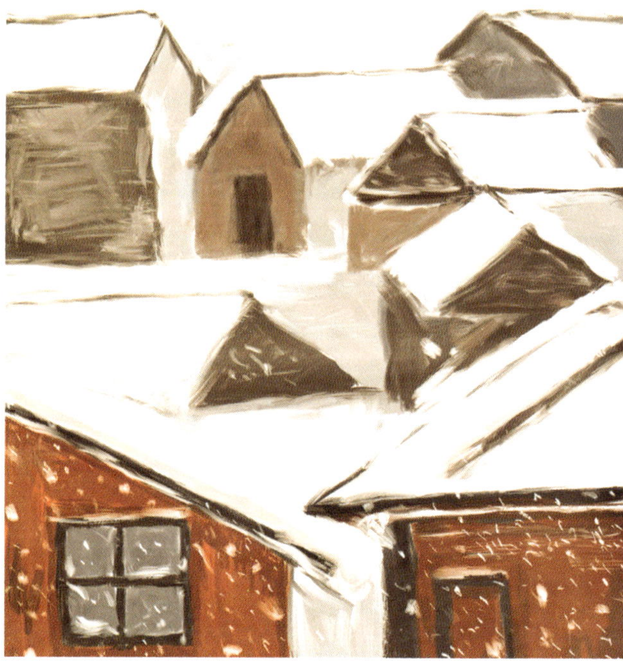

how he could help. The friend wrote back, 'Putins come and go. If you want to help, send us some poems and essays. We are putting together a literary magazine.' Kaminsky wrote: 'And, that is in the middle of the war. Imagine.'

A video is doing the rounds. It shows a Ukrainian man in Berdyansk removing a mine. The caption that I saw for the video said: 'I'm sorry but there's no hopes of ever being able to occupy a country full of people who just pick up mines and move them while a lit Marlboro dangles from their lips.'

1 March 2022

Twenty or thirty years ago, certainly fifty years ago, a diary of quotations would be made up of what the writer had read in books or newspapers. Perhaps even letters. Now, so much of my reading is online. My diary is made up of scraps I've collected from the internet. I'm not complaining, nor inviting anyone else to complain. It is just an observation. Today, I came across a quote from Nirmal Verma's novel *Ve Din* (Those Days):

> नहीं, सुख होता नहीं सिर्फ याद किया जा सकता है अपनी यातना में ... जब तुम्हें अचानक पता चलता है यह जून है, वह जनवरी था (No, you never really experience happiness, you can only recall it when you are unhappy ... When you suddenly realize this is June, and it was January then.)

2 March 2022

Brondesbury. A slight drizzle but it had stopped when Zadie Smith appeared. She was walking down the narrow pavement, framed by an overhanging branch of white cherry blossoms. Tall, dressed in black, slash of red lipstick. She is so beautiful. My students followed us to the street where Smith's story 'Embassy of Cambodia' is set. En route, she pointed to a three-storeyed brick building ('Fun autobiographical fact, that is the council flat where I grew up') and I'm not sure how many of the students even turned to look. I later thought maybe it wasn't a lack of curiosity, maybe it was just that it is easy to be dazed in Zadie's presence. We sat in a café after our tour and talked. She told my students that while they were expensively educated, Fatou and Andrew in her story were not. Not everyone in the world is educated. How to give their views and opinions a place in fiction? If having the right opinion would be the criterion for earning a part in fiction, Zadie said, then every twenty-two-year-old liberal arts student would be the perfect subject of fiction. I was thankful that she said this because I feel, though I hope I'm wrong, that our students expect literature to deliver the correct view of the world rather than something corrupted by real life.

3 March 2022

Yesterday, I had taken the overground to Richmond for the meeting with Zadie. The yellow of the train reminded me of a line from Vincent van Gogh: 'How wonderful yellow is. It stands for the sun.' Where was the line from? Had he written it in a letter? An online search revealed that he had indeed written it in a letter to his brother Theo on 12 August 1888. (Also included in the letter are lines about beauty and sexuality.) While searching for the source of the lines about yellow, I remembered that there had been some speculation about van Gogh suffering from a malady that affected his colour choices. What was it? On one site, the following:

> He might have suffered from xanthopsia, also known as 'yellow vision', as a result of digitalis intoxication. This theory is based on his having twice painted his doctor holding a foxglove (digitalis) plant, which was commonly used in the latter part of the nineteenth century to treat epilepsy. … Others believe that the shift in van Gogh's colour palette was simply influenced by his move to Paris in 1886 where it was generally assumed that he was inspired by the bold use of colour by the French Impressionists. And many have also wondered whether van Gogh simply used more yellow when he moved to the sunnier climes of Arles and Saint-Rémy because the weather meant he naturally spent more time outdoors and literally saw the world bathed in yellow sun.

4 March 2022

Mona got a call saying that Abbu had gone for his regular check-up in Toronto and was told that he

Overland to Richmond London, 2022

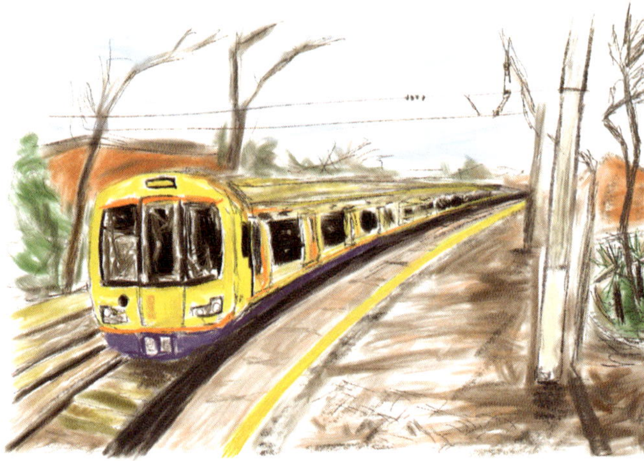

Overground to Richmond

needed a triple bypass heart surgery. He was being kept in the hospital for tests. We were going to have dinner tonight at the home of my former student Caleb's father and stepmother. Understandably, Mona didn't want to go. She wanted to be near the phone. In the end, I went by myself. It was pleasant to visit the beautiful home in Notting Hill, and for me to reflect on the luck through which some students become your friends. And in Caleb's case, even collaborators.

5 March 2022

Mona was quiet. The cousins like to hang out together and so I took Rahul and Sophia on the bus to Kensington Gardens and bought them an expensive Italian meal. During the journey and at the restaurant, I worked on a drawing on the iPad in response to the poems by Naveen Kishore that I had read on the

Tube last night. The poems are about the violence in Kashmir. I was reading the lines 'elsewhere / the sound / of bare feet / running'. Sitting next to me in the train was a family conversing in sign language. A young woman seated next to me, a young man with a steady, penetrating gaze (little hearing devices behind his ear) across from us, and next to the man a little girl who would make demonstrative shapes with her fingers to speak to the woman beside me and then make aargh-aargh noises. Anyway, sitting next to them as I read the poems, and particularly those words, I wondered how I would paint an elsewhere with the sound of bare feet running.

7 March 2022

Dushko asked me to make recordings on my phone for his podcast. I'm to talk about my daily practice. In the morning, I listen to what is being said on the meditation app on my phone. Just for a few minutes, to become conscious of my breath. For the past few days, I have been listening also to Pandit Kumar Gandharva singing nirgun bhajans.

At 8 a.m, when Rahul leaves for school, I sit down to write the morning pages. I always try to get the writing done right away. My quota of a hundred and fifty words, but anything more too. When I have completed my quota, I make a small check mark on the back page of whatever notebook I'm using at that time.

Before lunch, maybe a bit of exercise, just to keep the lower back problem at bay. Also, knee exercises. For the past week I have gone back to doing surya namaskar. If I start doing a drawing instead then the exercise gets pushed till later, just before I start cooking. Each day in London, I have stuck to the routine of doing a daily drawing. I also explain in one of the recordings that I record the passage of hours, sometimes even half-hours, in a planner. Which is to say, my planner records all the things I describe above.

At night, before going to bed, I make additional journal entries, and these are also sources on which I'm going to draw upon to write 'The Yellow Book'.

8 March 2022

After a late breakfast, went to the Royal Academy of Art to meet John Christie. We went to the Francis Bacon show with John's fellow artist Martin Battye. All that fascination with darkness and gore in Bacon's work but what was as interesting to me was his reliance on photographs taken by others. The curator has paired many of Bacon's paintings with small photographs that served as sources (several of them studies by Eadweard Muybridge—a dog, men wrestling, a disabled child). I liked Bacon's fidelity to realism and, simultaneously, the imaginative distortion he introduced in the images he painted. Martin said, 'Others use photographs as a kind of framework for painting, while for Bacon it was a springboard.'

I asked John and Martin questions about what was interesting about the paintings and their arrangement. John offered a quote from Bacon: 'I don't want to avoid telling a story, but I want very much to do the thing that Valery said—to give the sensation without the boredom of its conveyance. The moment the story enters the boredom comes upon you.' What are the implications for writing? Not just the absence of creaky plots but even narrative. Don't tell me how you arrived at the story. In fact, don't even start on a story. Offer me only sensations.

Map of reading. Other titles spotted on the London trains (I have so few titles to report because most people are only reading things on their phones): *The Lost Café Schindler* by Meriel Schindler; *This Charming Man* by C.K. McDonnell; *Who Am I, Again?* by Lenny Henry; *Homie* by Danez Smith.

This has been a week of rejections: a book proposal, a mixed-media piece for a magazine, and a fellowship application. Every no carries an echo in this deep valley of despair where I stand, a small figure in the dark. And then all the hurt and melodrama fades. For a few days, I waver between entering a mindset where I expect further rejections and only rejections—and then, for a change, thinking that once these rejections are out of the way, the season will change, there will be fresh winds, shining vistas. The fact is that there is always new work to do. It is the work that matters. So much calmness in that knowledge.

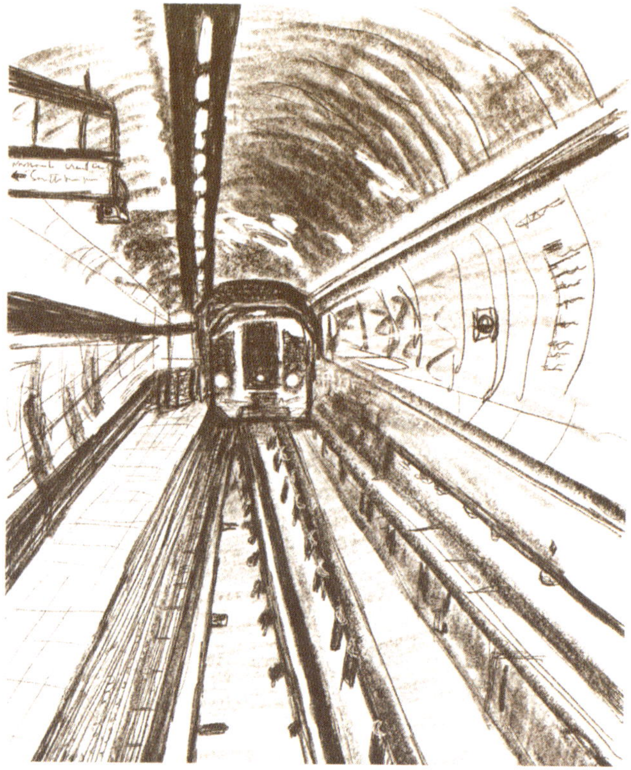

Victoria Line,
Euston Station,
London, 2022

9 March 2022

I was on my way to our class meeting with Ian Jack when something terrible happened. I was waiting on the platform at Euston Tube station for the northbound Victoria Line train. I was going to take the train only for two stops before getting off at Highbury Islington. From the end of the platform, sudden noises. I remember that when I had looked up last, the lighted electric sign had said that the train to Walthamstow Central was due in one minute. Then shouts: four or five people down the platform, one or two of them waving their arms. The light from the train's engine was visible at the mouth of the tunnel. Then I saw him. Middle-aged, or maybe even older, bald, bespectacled. How long would I have seen him—for a second, maybe two. I was running towards him, my arms outstretched. A futile gesture. The train was upon him in a flash.

Two women in hijabs covered their faces. A man had turned his head away, his hands covering his ears. But I was watching. When the train hit him, there was a small explosion—like a large balloon or a bag filled with air bursting. A fine spray of blood, red vapour that floated down the length of the platform. There was no sign of the man who had been killed.

I went to the older woman in the hijab. She was crying. She said she didn't know how the man had got on the tracks. Everyone else too had only caught sight of him as the train came. I was sure I had seen the man trying to climb back on to the platform. Half an hour later, I wasn't sure about what I had seen. Had the man actually jumped down and at the moment I had caught sight of him he was simply turning his face away from the rushing train?

The train stood still, its doors not opening. A young man in a blue jacket, a thatch of black hair on his face, suddenly appeared among us on the platform, loudly asking what had happened. I told him. Everyone leave the station. Out. I'm a police officer. His hand was now on a button on the wall and a bell started ringing. Outside, I approached another police officer, this one in uniform, and told him what I had seen. He asked me if I was okay and I said I was. Half an hour later, I began to feel sick, vomit rising in my throat.

Opening my journal, I wrote down what I had seen. And it was in writing these details down that I revised my earlier sense that the man was trying to get back on the platform. Why had I formed that opinion? Maybe because I had seen a video of a man who had fallen down on the New York subway and another man, a stranger, had pulled him up just in time. I had, in that sudden moment when I first saw the doomed man on the track, responded to that memory. In my rush to save him, I hadn't noticed how unhurried he had appeared in his movements and gestures. His motives, just like his identity, would remain a mystery and likely haunt me for a very long time.

On the way back from class, I went to the platform where the man had been killed. About twenty or thirty feet away, a couple stood talking. Someone had dropped cookies near where I was, they were scattered on the ground and a few had been crushed underfoot. There was no sign of what had happened earlier in the day.

10 March 2022

Class yesterday was held in Canonbury Pub, once frequented by George Orwell. Ian Jack took me to the flat where Orwell had lived during 1944–47. In class, Ian told my students that he had never known 'such an apprehensive time' as the one created by the war in Ukraine. 'This crisis has sucked all the air.' Not even Covid had posed such a big danger of annihilation. Had my students anticipated this war and what were

The Writer's Place, London, 2022

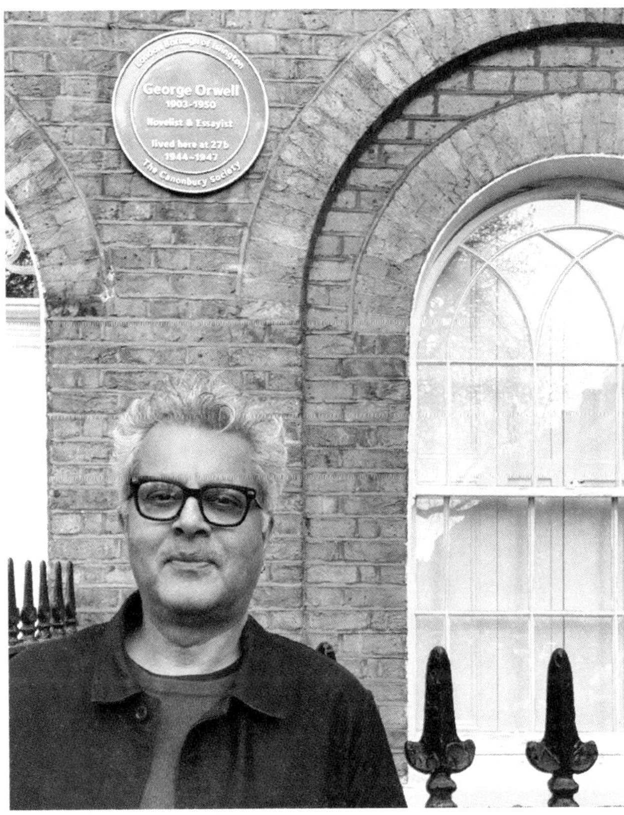

their thoughts? One student said that she had planned to go to Poland but her father had warned her, weeks ago, of the approaching war. 'But if you had gone,' Ian said, 'you would have had something to write about.' Which is exactly what any writer should say to a younger writer.

Ian said that when he was young he wanted to be a writer but didn't know what to write about. He went to a particular railway station in Glasgow and wrote about four hundred words. Somebody who read the piece said that something has to happen to make it work. You have to ask what happened, you have to ask why. You have to think in terms of character and location. Ian said, 'You have to insert yourself into a situation and you need to have an imagination.'

In not turning my eye away from what happened yesterday at Euston station, I was inserting myself into a situation. And the situation then entered my imagination. When Rahul was leaving for school this morning, a panic seized me. I said to him, 'Stand behind the yellow line.' Be careful. I looked online but there was nothing beyond a small mention of a death on the tracks. Obviously, nothing about the man's identity. Last night when I lay down to sleep, the scene I had witnessed replayed in my head. I shut my eyes and the red cloud I had sighted floated above my eyelids.

11 March 2022

Meanwhile, life goes on. Arundhati Roy has been awarded the St Louis Literary Award. Last night, I spoke for an hour on Zoom about Roy's work and the ways in which my own writing is in dialogue with it. I had read the first page of *The God of Small Things* several times before writing a passage about rain in *A Time Outside This Time*. One of the first things I

Meanwhile, Life Goes On, London, 2022

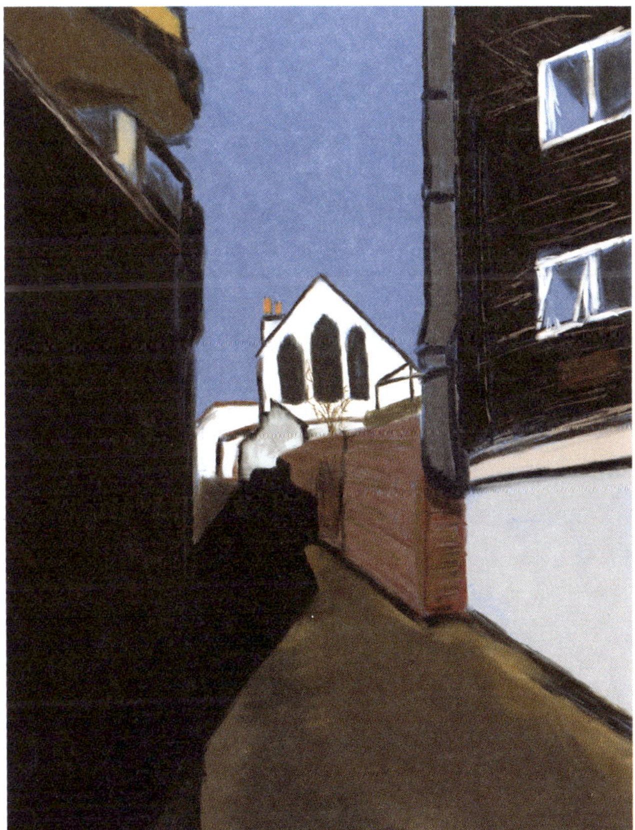

told the small audience was that Macaulay's Minute on Education in 1835, introducing the teaching of English in India, was meant to produce a nation of clerks. Instead, we became writers.

I had said something similar to Arundhati once. And she said that she didn't want to blame Macaulay alone. 'There is something clerky and calculating about our privileged classes. They see themselves as the State or as advisors to the State …' The real point I wanted to make during my Zoom talk was that politics is the elephant in the room of literature. It takes so much space that, as in the Kay Ryan poem about the

Hampstead Miniature, London, 2022

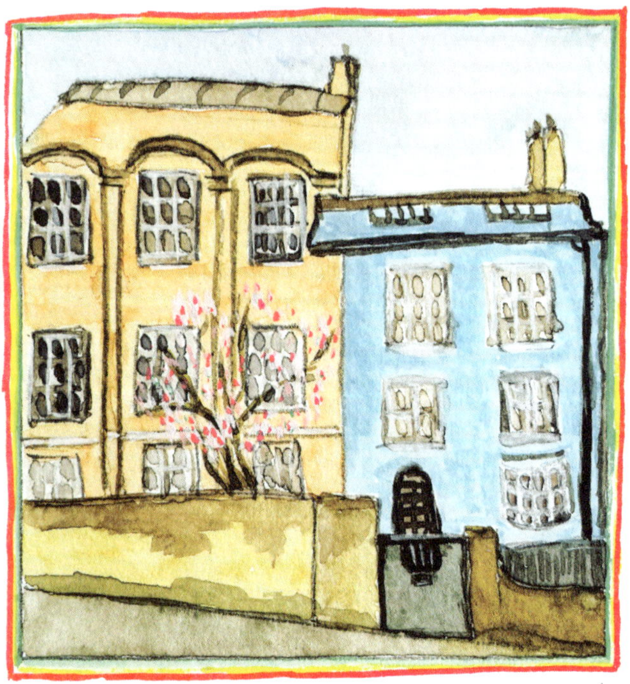

elephant in the room, there is no room to talk about it. But the thing about Arundhati, who is always political, is that her style, her exuberant and excessive language, turns the elephant into a mouse.

12 March 2022

Ila didn't want to spend her visit in London. Mona has taken both kids to Paris.

Late at night, I sent the letter to Chiki that I had written in my head so many weeks ago but beginning with: 'It has taken me some time to gather courage to write this, and please forgive this intrusion …'

Dinner at Ian's. Before class the other day, I had told him what had happened earlier that afternoon at the Euston station. I also told him tonight that I had been back at the station since. He didn't think it was a good idea. I couldn't explain, and as there were other guests, we dropped the subject. An instinct in me, a writer's instinct, had made me watch what had happened: I had seen something horrible, and now I could not unsee it. I didn't tell Ian that every time I've been back at the platform, my heart seizes and it all seems to turn dark. I have so many questions. Not just who was the man, or what had his day or week or year been like, but also, and this might be disturbing to some, how and over what period did he plan those last few minutes. I stare into the darkness of that tunnel.

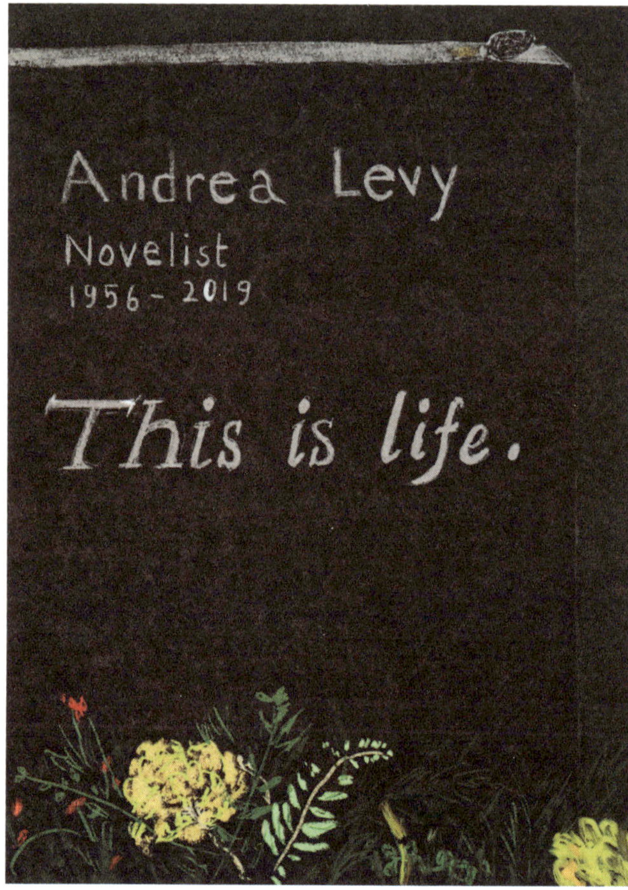

Andrea Levy's Gravestone, Highgate Cemetery, London, 2022

13 March 2022

Listening on Audible to Andrew O'Hagan reading his novel *Mayflies*. It is a moving novel about a friend's joyful life and his death but I'm also impressed by O'Hagan's masterful reading. Such comic range.

A video of Vinod Kumar Shukla is doing the rounds on social media. Here is one of the best writers in India but he has received only a pittance in royalties over the years. Outright theft by his Hindi language publishers. Even his protest as he speaks to the camera has the simplicity and unbetrayable elegance of all his writings.

15 March 2022

Took the class to the National Theatre to watch a performance of Andrea Levy's *Small Island*. I had taught the novel in an earlier version of the Black London course, but I liked the show even more. Partly because of the exceptional staging, the tight choreography of the presentation, and how the work seemed to involve so many bodies and was, therefore, a representation of a community. The students said that they had been uncertain when they heard the show ran for three hours but the time had passed quickly. When it was over, we came out and saw the buildings on the other side of the Thames bathed in the bright blue and yellow of the Ukraine flag. There was also a note from Pat saying that there was a review of *A Time Outside This Time* in the *Times Literary Supplement* calling the book 'an anatomy of deceit'. The line that Pat had quoted from the TLS was the following one: 'Kumar navigates the mists of contemporary deception with a penetrating intelligence and keen sense of paradox.' I always feel that if you don't want to be affected by the insane reviews—not always malicious, but often written in bad faith—you should also stay distant from the positive reviews. But I confess to feeling good about this one.

16 March 2022

Despite driving rain, most of the students in my class came to the V&A Museum where Deepa Anappara spoke about how she wrote a story after seeing the 'Tippoo's Tiger' display there. Fiction as a corrective to the colonial archive. Then we walked to Taymour Soomro's Kensington apartment to discuss his story of queer love, 'Oskar in Five Parts'. At one point, I read aloud a few lines from the story: 'The Victoria Line is empty and cool. Someone has left a newspaper on the seat beside you. There's water on the moon. Frank Sinatra died. *Citizen Kane* is the best film of all time. You think of Oskar's broad, golden back. You think of pressing his cheek to your shoulder.' What

Spring Comes at Night, London, 2022

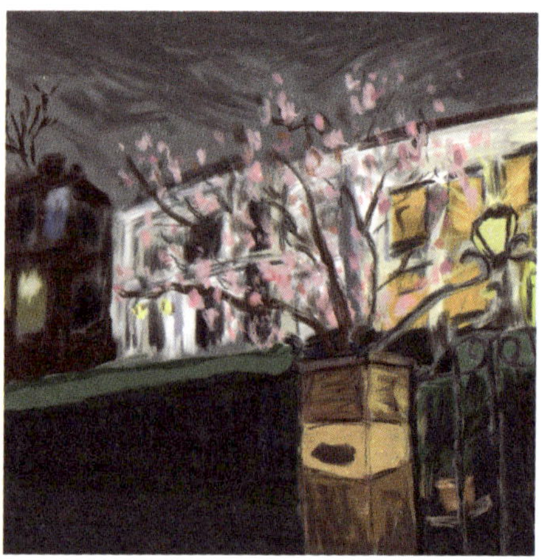

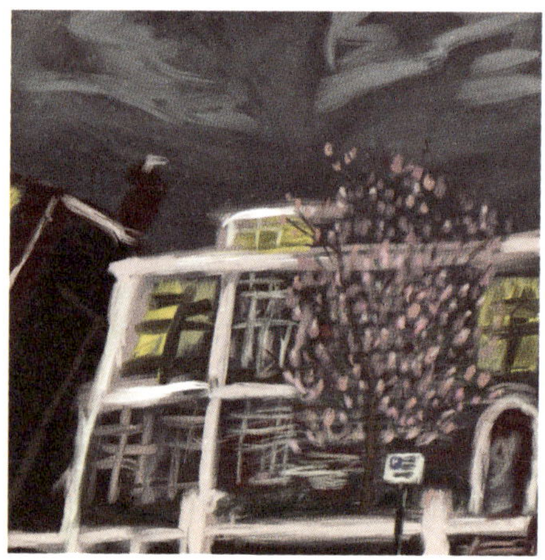

an extraordinary list, giving a quick sense of the time and milieu where the story is set. I asked Taymour to now engage in 'bad writing' and take away all the delicacy from the telling. He laughed, unable to come up with anything. I persisted. He said, 'You wanted to have sex with Oskar so you took the Tube to see him.' Taymour and Deepa spoke to the students about their edited anthology, *Letters to a Writer of Color*. 'We asked ourselves what your creative writing class would be like if all your faculty were people of colour?' I'm a contributor to that collection. Dinner with the students and the two writers at Tayyab's in Brick Lane. On the long train ride back the fear that my co-passengers could smell on my coat the spices from the restaurant.

17 March 2022

As it is my birthday today and the sun was out, I gave myself a present. Rather than worry about writing, I started the day by making a painting. Gouache instead of making it on the iPad because there was a sense of leisure built into the act. The same tree that I see on Heath Street on the way to the Hampstead Tube station. Dinner with Saad and Ayesha at a Persian place called Kateh. Worried about the absences from class and the sluggishness of the work done by students on their journals, I sent a harsh note asking them basically to do the bare fucking minimum.

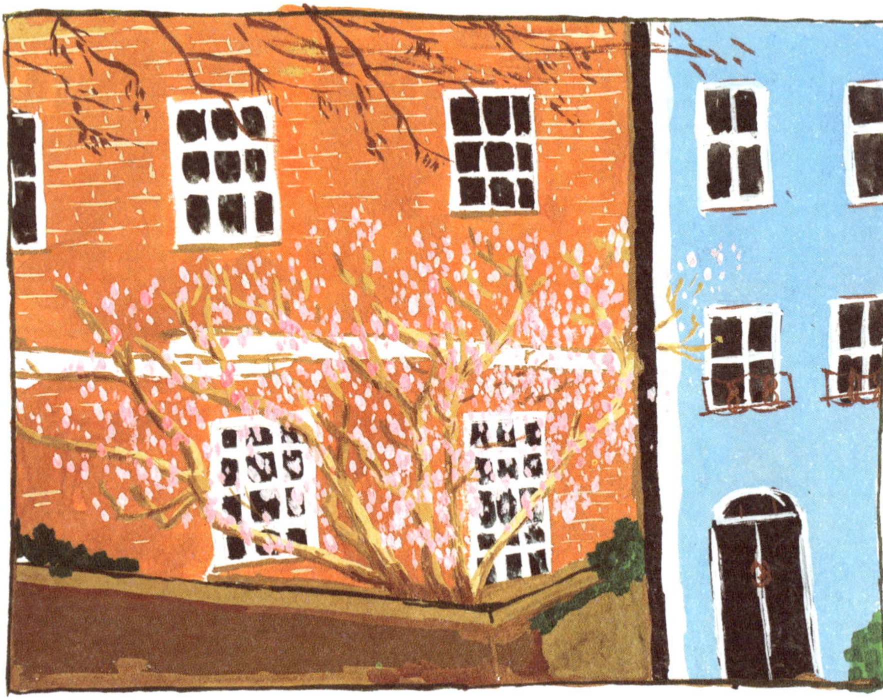

Birthday Present, London, 2022

18 March 2022

Started reading *Moby Dick* in the online group with Yiyun. There are other things I need to do urgently, including possibly supplying blurbs for two books and certainly sending out a tenure letter by 25 March, but it is embarrassing that I've never read this big book. And Yiyun's readings are so uniquely hers, I want to be a part of that daily conversation. There was a tweet with a photograph today from A Public Space: Yiyun is copying out *Moby Dick* by hand, 'the epitome of slow reading and savouring every word'.

19 March 2022

Took my students to Margate. Read *Moby Dick* on the train. It was a hurried trip and mildly disappointing because I didn't have time to take in everything on offer at the Turner Contemporary. We did get the chance to eat fish and chips in a restaurant near the beach. Upon return, at St Pancras International, saw

Margate Minute, London, 2022

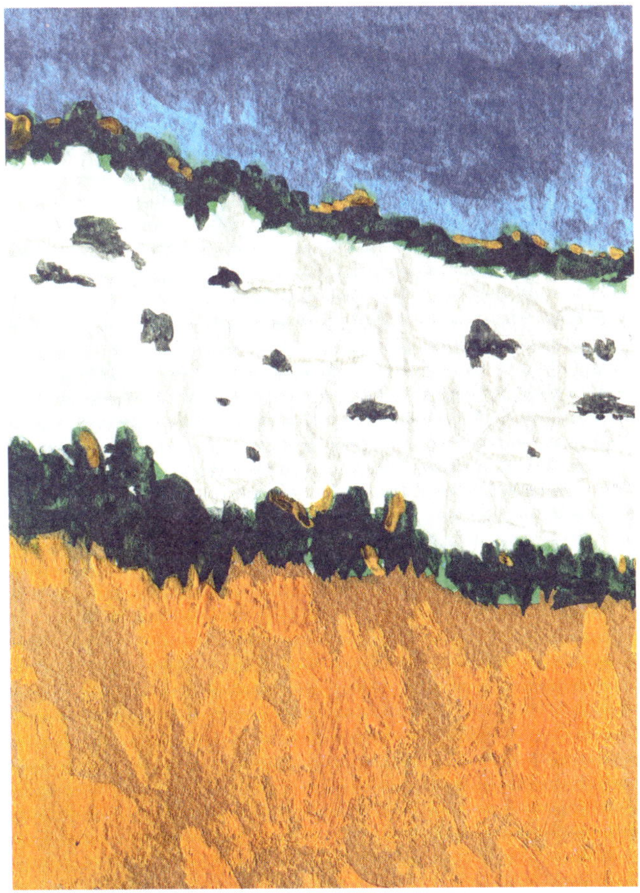

transport workers holding signs in Ukrainian (one half yellow, one half blue) to welcome refugees.

20 March 2022

Ila had come out to the living room three or four days ago and asked me to look outside. The sky had a yellow hue. I didn't give it much thought but today I came across a news item about the dust from the Sahara. I then noticed that the kitchen windowsill has a layer of red dust on the white paint.

One of my students was instructed by her therapist to focus on one small thing in the city as a way of keeping anxiety at bay. Maybe she could track a colour. My student has chosen red. But red dust blowing across Europe all the way from the Sahara … this thought might only lead to further anxiety in someone's mind.

24 March 2022

We have two more classes left this term. My dear friend and Vassar colleague Heesok Chang flew across the Atlantic to teach today's class. He talked about the figure of the flâneur and the related figure of the collector walking through the urban streets. The students were required to collect over the space of a few days four objects that caught their eye. Heesok brought his artist-friend Julia Miranda to the class; Julia made a painting for each student based on their collection. A keepsake from their time in London. The students had collected small items that meant something to them: a flower, a playing card, a bubblegum wrapper, a cheap brooch purchased from a thrift store, a ticket. They were concrete items, a list of things. I think Heesok was looking for a mood, rather, a thought, that united these disparate things. Upon returning to the flat after class, I decided that I would ask my students to produce a paragraph about their collection or, better still, about the drawing each one received today. This paragraph would be modelled after this glorious passage from Sam Selvon's *The Lonely Londoners*:

> The changing of the seasons, the cold slicing winds, the falling leaves, sunlight on green grass, snow on the land, London particular. Oh what it is and where it is and why it is, no one knows, but to have said: 'I walked on Waterloo Bridge,' 'I rendezvoused at Charing Cross,' 'Piccadilly Circus is my playground,' to say these things, to have lived these things, to have lived in the great city of London, centre of the world. To one day lean against the wind walking up the Bayswater Road (destination unknown), to see the leaves swirl and dance and spin on the pavement (sight unseeing), to write a casual letter home beginning: 'Last night in Trafalgar Square …'

26 March 2022

I have been reading this small volume of Virginia Woolf's essays called *Oh, to Be a Painter!* The title comes from an essay in which Woolf pits writing against painting. 'But words, words! How inadequate you are! How weary one gets of you! How you will always be saying too much or too little! Oh to be silent! Oh to be a painter!' (No comma in the quote, but it is there in the title of the book I have been reading.) When Woolf celebrates 'the silent kingdom of paint', it is important to remember that she has also noted the 'zone of silence in the middle of every art'. (She doesn't want narrative in painting: 'A story-telling picture is as pathetic as and ludicrous as a trick played by a dog ...') Here are her words of praise for her sister Vanessa Bell's paintings: 'Mrs Bell is as silent as the grave. Her pictures do not betray her. Their reticence is inviolable. That is why they intrigue and draw us on ...' Surely what is being said here about paintings would also hold true, in Woolf's mind, about literature and about praising the sort of literature that has an expressiveness beyond words.

What interested me most were Woolf's remarks in an essay on the artist Walter Sickert, particularly when she writes of the way in which 'the arts are closely united'. She attributes 'the starved condition of criticism' in her time to the fact that critics have focused on what is in print and not considered how words are in conversation with music and painting. She praises Sickert as a 'hybrid' artist. Who is a hybrid? The latter, the raiders, in this mode of classification laid out by Woolf: 'Some, that is to say, bore deeper and deeper into the stuff of their own art; others are always making raids into the lands of others.' I want to proclaim my allegiance to the nation of hybrids!

28 March 2022

Last week of class. I was on the Tube today and wrote in my notebook about the drawing that was made for me in Heesok's class last Thursday:

> During Christmas holiday at a dear friend's, maybe five or six years ago, I had watched the film *Mr Turner* directed by Mike Leigh. I liked the film; it was about a passion for art but also about passion grounded in superb contradictions. Turner became a figure of even greater interest to me when I began drawing. In the film I had seen him going to Margate to sketch and paint. And now, after arriving in London (in late December I had gone to the National Gallery to look at his paintings), I bought a postcard showing one of his sea paintings and I pasted it on my kitchen shelf. Then, several weeks later, I went to Margate with my students. We visited Turner Contemporary. This seaside structure appears on the British twenty-pound note. In Margate, at the Turner Contemporary, I bought another postcard, this one of a local beach scene, with fishing baskets, that Turner had painted. When Heesok asked us to collect four items and share it in class for his friend Julia to draw, I chose my two Turner postcards and a twenty-pound note from my wallet. What would my fourth object be? I had a coaster from a pub in Islington named Compton Arms. Pearl,

our programme assistant, had been a bartender there. Also, it had been one of George Orwell's favourites and is regarded as one of the three Canonbury pubs that served as the inspiration for his fictional (and also ideal) watering hole named The Moon Under Water. During the years 1944–47, Orwell had lived around the corner from the Compton Arms. ('The Moon Under Water' had been written in 1946.) As I have told my students, probably more than once, Orwell was born in Motihari, close to my ancestral village in Bihar. (When I tweeted a photograph of myself standing outside Orwell's Canonbury home, a blue plaque behind me, someone commented: 'How did I not know that Orwell was born in India? My whole life has been a lie!') These affiliations, artistic and political, brought to the surface by my stay in London, were drawn together in this artwork. That's what also happens in great cities: meetings, conjunctions, a drawing together of forces. And always, the arrival of the new.

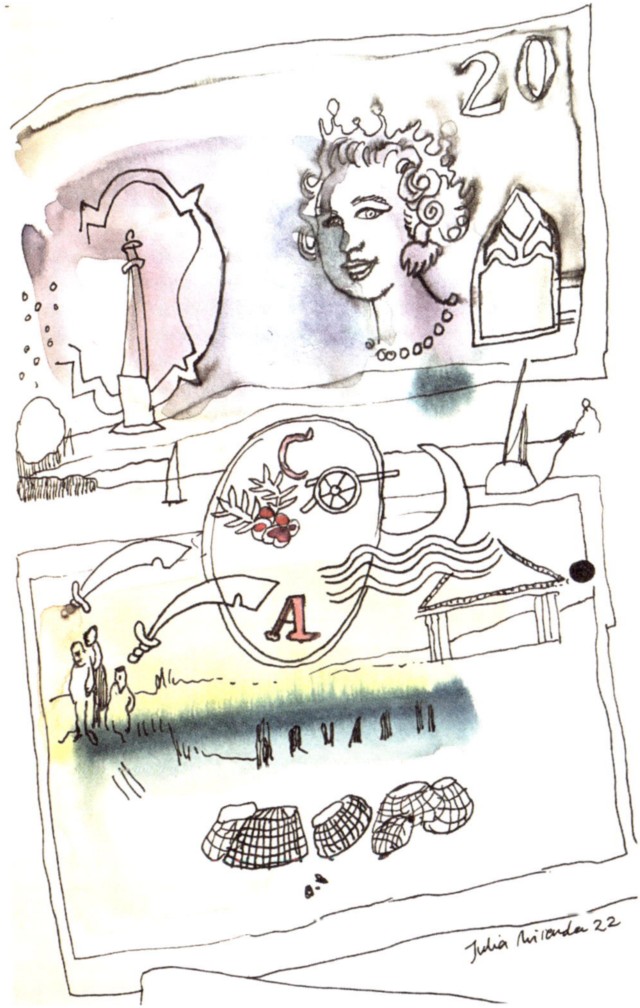

Mr Turner
and Mr Orwell,
London, 2022

Host Country/Lost Country

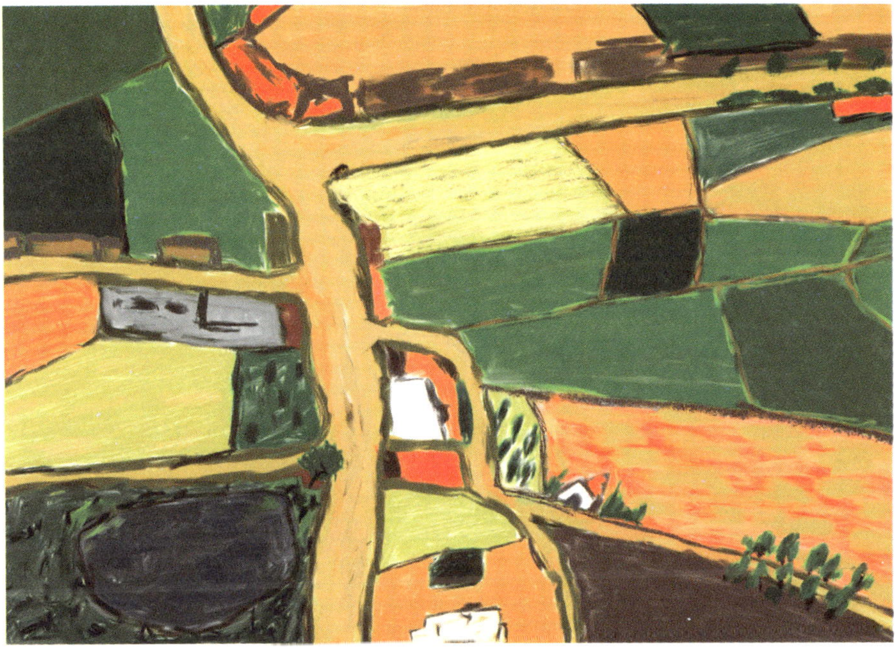

Remembered Village, London, 2022

Amarjit Chandan is a Punjabi poet who was born in Nairobi, Kenya, a year prior to India's independence. He is now in his late seventies. When he was very young, a boy of eight, Chandan's parents returned from Africa to Punjab. Chandan's father had worked as a photographer but he was also a revolutionary. In his politics, Chandan followed in his father's footsteps. In 1971, he was arrested for anti-state activities and spent two years in prison. In 1980, Chandan moved to England where he worked as a translator and wrote poetry.

A friend had sent me a link to a video which had been made in April, 2016—it showed Chandan and John Berger in the latter's home in France. Chandan reads his poem 'Gunachaur' in Punjabi. Then, Berger reads the translation of the poem into English by Julia Casterton.

Gunachaur

I have never been to Gunachaur.
When I hear the word Gunachaur
something happens to me.

Mother used to talk about her distant relations
living in Gunachaur.
I used to fly there on her wings.

I felt—
Gunachaur is a place
somewhere beyond Jalandhar
near Nawān Shahar.
A light flickers in darkness seen from above.
I imagined the relations I never met.

Even now that place is not far off
It's near, quite near
Wherever I happen to be
My mother is with me
and Gunachaur is close by.

When I came back to my flat in Hampstead after my meeting with Chandan, I translated his poem into Hindi because I wanted to be a part of the conversation:

गुणाचौर

गुणाचौर मैं कभी नहीं गया
कोई गुणाचौर का नाम लेता है
तो दिल में कुछ होने लगता है।

माँ जब गुणाचौर में रहने वाले
अपने रिश्तेदारों की बातें किया करती थी
और मैं उसके पंखों पे सवार गुणाचौर चला जाता।

मुझे लगता—
गुणाचौर कोई जगह है
कहीं जालंधर के पास
नवांशहर के परे।
मैं देखता जैसे
ऊपर आसमान से दिखाई देती
बत्ती है
जलती-बुझती
मैं उन रिश्तेदारों के बारे में सोचता
जिनसे कभी मिला नहीं।

आज भी वह जगह दूर नहीं
पास ही है, बहुत पास
मैं जहाँ भी होता हूँ
वहीं होती है माँ
और वहीं होता है गुणाचौर।

I had been reading an essay by Chandan on the subject of translation just minutes before I met him outside London's Ealing Tube station. In that essay, a poet named Ravil Bukharev had told Chandan that in London he struggles with German. But the language comes back to him when he is in Germany because there 'even the trees speak German'. I had liked that phrase of Bukharev's. In response, Chandan said that whenever he hears a dhol or drum—wherever in the world he might be—he believes the drum is speaking Punjabi.

In a café, I asked Chandan about Gunachaur. Is it a fixed place, a real place, in his imagination? I was thinking of those who have roots—even while what they really have are routes—but Chandan very quickly disabused me of this notion. He reminded me that he had said in his poem that he had never been to Gunachaur. It wasn't his ancestral village, only some distant relatives lived there. He liked the sound its name made: his mother used to talk about it, and the music of that name had found a place in his heart. 'I have not gone to that place,' he said to me in Hindi, 'but I am always there.'

Why had the poem moved me so? I wanted Chandan to answer this question. He said that the word 'Ma', the sound that it made, invoked a relationship that is so much more powerful for us than it is for the people in the West. He insisted on this. He said, 'You do not give a sigh when you think of your mother in English.'

Did I look sceptical? He said that there are words in one language that do not exist in another. 'I miss you' and 'I love you' are words so often spoken in English but there isn't a close structural parallel in Hindi or Punjabi. He began talking of an essay by the eminent Hindi critic Hazari Prasad Dwivedi who argued that Hindi didn't have the word 'dhanyavaad', now customarily used as a way of delivering thanks, till the British came to India. This etiquette of constantly—and, Chandan seemed to be saying, insistently and even obsequiously—offering thanks wasn't present or required till the colonizers came to India. Or, for that matter, the practice of very quickly saying 'sorry' for everything in so light a way that it is routine and almost meaningless. Again, there is no such single word for that easy emotion in Hindi or Punjabi.

Chandan was now on a roll. He was saying that till the Christian missionaries landed among the Latin Americans, the latter had no word for 'sin'. I got up to get more tea for Chandan. When I sat down again, he asked me to tell him what my favourite word in Hindi was. The first one that came to mind was 'aanchal'. I had in mind what is referred to as the loose end of the sari that hangs off the shoulder, and it came to me probably because I was aware that there wouldn't perhaps be an easily translated word for it in English. I asked Chandan to offer me his own examples. He said 'nikka' in Punjabi for something small; another word was 'telephone', as pronounced in Punjabi ('telefoon'), denoting the loud ringing of a machine sitting in a room.

Throughout our conversation, we had been speaking of John Berger and the kind of influence he had wielded on both of us and how much we owed him: Chandan said that he had first read Berger's *A Seventh Man* and was hugely influenced by it. He sent Berger his poems. Once, in a film that was being made about his life, Berger read out a poem of Chandan's in translation ('Lahsan' in Punjabi, meaning 'Garlic'), and later, at an event where Berger was speaking, Chandan had gone up to him and introduced himself. A friendship was born.

Then, Chandan came across a phrase of Berger's: 'whispering to the faded ink of father's writing'. Inspired by that line, Chandan wrote a poem titled 'To Father'. When he first read that poem, Chandan told me, Berger had 'tears in his eyes'. Seated in the café in front of Chandan, I opened his book of poems, *Sonata for Four Hands*. I began reading 'To Father' out loud. Chandan later sent me the photograph mentioned in the poem—the father with his eyes shut, cheek pressed against Chandan who was a little boy at that time. '*Where are you now father? Can you take some time off from death?*' In the café, as I read out the poem, my voice caught. I was afraid I would start crying but I kept reading. Chandan had written, '*The photograph doesn't show the lump in your throat.*' I had been thinking of Berger with tears in his eyes, and I feared that I was imitating him, as I had done in my writing. And then I thought of my father, who was eighty-six. Maybe I thought of my son too, who was a bit older than Chandan was in that picture, and who often pressed his cheek against mine. I can't remember. What I remember is that I was crying but I did finish reading the poem.

An Old Photograph, London, 2022

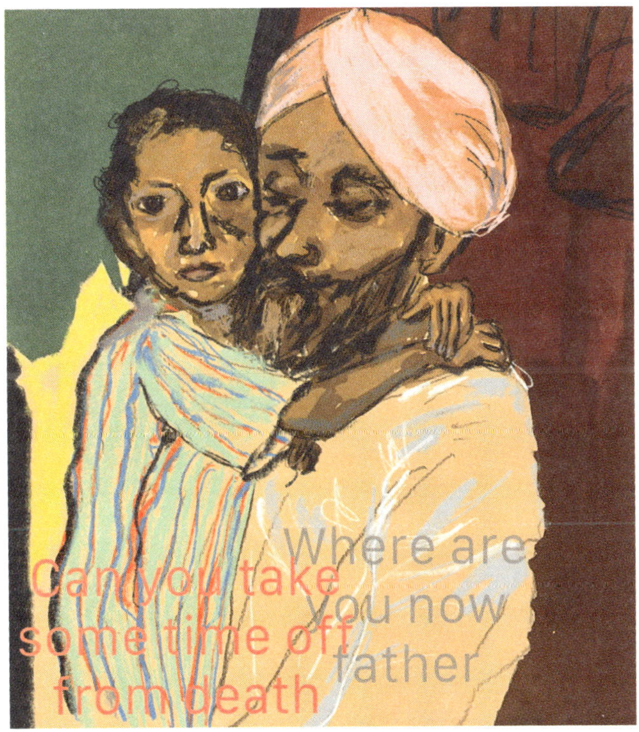

June 2022

A few weeks after my meeting with Chandan I went to India to visit my father in Patna. In the plane from

Delhi, poor migrant workers returning home for Eid from Saudi Arabia and other countries in the Gulf. Because I was speaking in Urdu, they assumed I was Muslim. How long had it been since I had come home? I said two years and more. I was going to see my father, I said. One of them, the older one, said that my return would make this a special Eid for my father.

My father, probably because of social isolation, has aged terribly during the pandemic. I would try to talk to him on the phone, calling him from New York or London, and he appeared lethargic and uninterested. In early April, I bought two tickets to India. One for myself and one for my son. My son loves to talk to his grandfather; both of them possess a fantastic memory for trivia. But then my son's application for a visa for India was denied. We were told that the Ministry of Home Affairs would need at least four to six weeks to do a security check. This is because his mother, my wife, was born in Pakistan.

Like so many of my friends from school in Patna and Delhi, my father, who had always appeared liberal to me, had become a Modi supporter. What did he think of the Indian government regarding his twelve-year-old grandson with suspicion? When I got home from the airport in the late afternoon, my father was lying in bed. I touched his feet. He looked older, even shrunken, and vulnerable. He asked me about my children, what their plans were and when they would be able to visit him. I didn't ask the question I

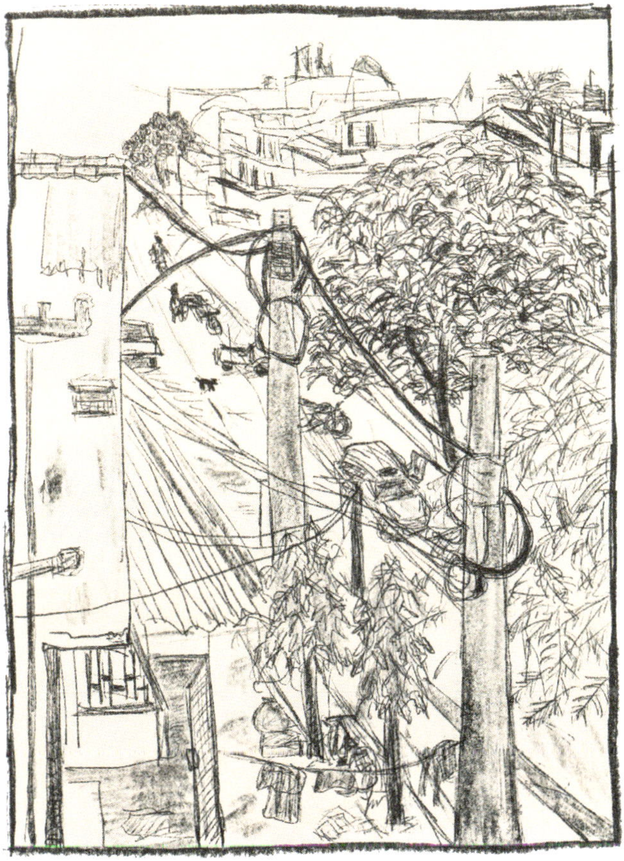

Below My Sister's Kitchen, Patna, Bihar, 2022

had been framing on the flight. In fact, I knew that I wouldn't even bring up Modi's name. We were going to be together for only five days.

My father liked to take a walk in the morning for twenty minutes but preferred to lie in bed for the rest of the day. I don't know exactly why this should be so. The other day, on the flight from London, I had watched Anthony Hopkins in the film *The Father*. He is suffering from dementia, his memories are jumbled. He tells his nurse, 'I feel as if I'm losing all my leaves.' I put the movie on pause to note down the line in my notebook. There was a reason for the lump in my throat. My sister had informed me on the phone that recently my father, for the first time in his life, seemed disoriented. For someone who remembers everything, not just phone numbers but also other information like bank account numbers and registration plate numbers, he appeared lost. He was now mixing up dates of birth.

One morning, I told my father I was going for a walk on the new promenade beside the Ganga, and he said in response, quite correctly, that it was an auspicious day, Akshay Tritiya, the day celebrated as the one when the river Ganga was said to have left the heavens and descended to earth.

It was also Eid-ul-Fitr. On the Ganga promenade, there were young Muslim men strolling about in their new kurtas, mostly a blazing white but also yellow or pale blue. Although I had expected it to be hot, a fine breeze now lifted from the river. On occasion, my nose caught the smell of sewage and decay, but otherwise the air was pleasant. In news photographs of the promenade, I had seen students seated in long lines, cramming for exams, but there were very few of them now around. Young women posed for selfies at the water's edge. Four teens, two boys and two girls, were recording a TikTok video without any self-consciousness. My father had asked me to take a sip of the holy water but I saw the debris and the filth and didn't dare.

For fifty rupees, boats took you to the opposite bank, where you could walk on the sand and buy tea at one of the shacks. I went. Sweet milky tea was served in clay cups. When dusk fell, the lights of the city began

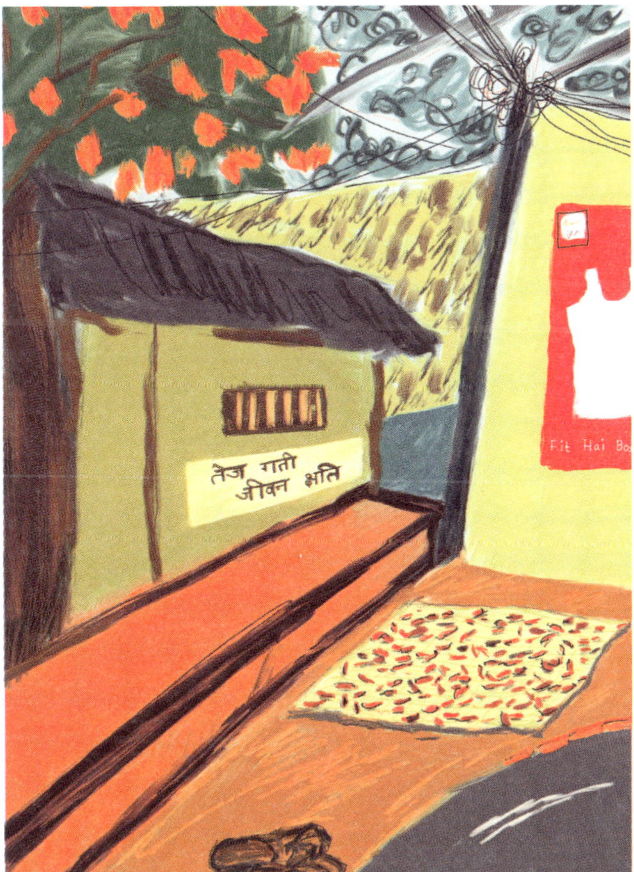

On the Road to My Village: Ad for Men's Vests. (And a speed warning in Hindi. Do all such warnings rhyme? In English, the sign said: 'Speed thrills but kills'.) Champaran, Bihar, 2022

to glitter in the distance. And the glowing fires where dead bodies were being cremated. On the boat back to the promenade, a small group of young men took it upon themselves to raise the slogan 'Jai Shri Ram'. Everyone on the boat watched the young men but didn't join in. On the way back to my father's house, before I had reached the open expanse of Gandhi Maidan, I looked up and saw, above the dusty haze of Ashok Rajpath, the thin and brilliant crescent of the Eid moon.

My father agreed to come on a day trip to our village in Champaran. I have dim memories of the smoke-blackened hut in which my father was born but, while I was still a boy, a brick house was built where the hut had stood. There was no electricity in the village till I was already in college. No running water either. When I was a growing up, the trip from Patna took a whole day, first crossing the Ganga by ferry, then a long journey by train or car, and, during the final stretch, even a bullock cart. But now it is possible to drive there in under four hours. My father is very proud of these changes.

If you were to go by the billboards on the drive from Patna to Muzaffarpur to Motihari, you would find the story of a nation under construction. Most advertisements are for cement, iron rods, tiles, pipes, paints. Another item that enjoys a similar ubiquity: coaching classes. Tuition for chemistry, mathematics, biology. Assurances of high scores in the entrance exams to engineering and medical colleges. And ads for men's underwear. Bollywood actors wearing vests or briefs. So, even in the hinterland, or particularly in the hinterland, signs of hectic construction, a desperation about making it in a transforming market, even if mobility seems limited only to the male consumer, confidently armoured in crisp white cotton.

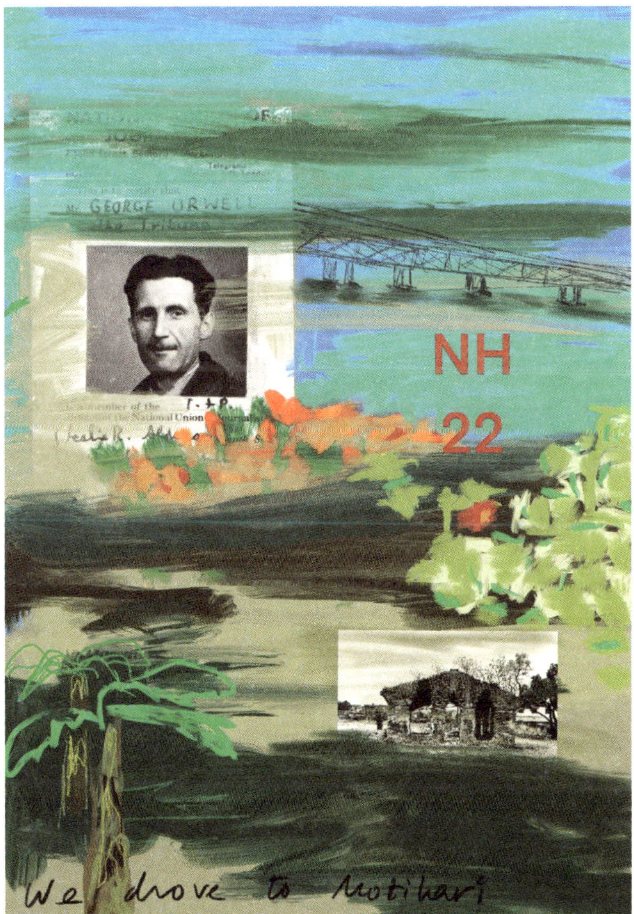

Opium Warehouse, Motihari, Bihar, 2022

On the way to our village was Motihari town and I wanted to visit George Orwell's birthplace. Orwell's father, Richard Blair, was a sub-deputy opium agent for the British. While he was still an infant, Orwell was taken by his mother to England. The house where he was born is now gone; a small house has been built at the site in Orwell's memory. A hundred yards away stand the skeletal ruins of the warehouse where the opium was stored by the British before being sent to China. There are no books or pictures in the two-room structure erected in Orwell's memory.

From Motihari, it was less than an hour's drive to our village, Jadopur. All through my childhood, this last leg of the trip, if it was made in a motor vehicle, left us covered in dust. Our clothes, faces, even our eyebrows would be coated in a grey dust that I had seen nowhere else. But now there is a narrow tar road leading right into the village. This isn't the biggest change, however. The most striking sight for me was two women riding scooters. And even more promising, girls in school uniforms on pink bicycles. The bicycles were provided free by the government in a bid to raise female literacy. My sense is that the policy is revolutionary: the free bicycles have brought women out of their homes in a rural, rigidly patriarchal society.

Our village home was clean but derelict, its rooms locked, and parts of the house already collapsed, a heap of bricks. I have a novel coming out in which I have put parts of that house—the prayer room where I imagined my grandmother's death; she died while I was in grad school in America and I wasn't there to witness it—and looking at those empty spaces now I felt I had stolen the soul of that place for my story. Feeling uncomfortable, I quickly stepped outside. A few of the villagers had stopped by. They had seen me on Ravish Kumar's show and wanted to send him a message. A quiet man whom I had never met before also wanted to talk to me. He had been appointed as a part of a government scheme for rural upliftment. His work was extremely local; he had his roots in the area; his official designation was 'vikas mitr' or 'development friend'. He had come to talk to me because he wanted me to write an op-ed asking for clinics in those parts of the villages where the primary inhabitants were people from the lower castes. There were no provisions for hygienic living in those poor areas. Villagers often fell ill due to the heat. Food spoiled easily on hot days and caused diarrhoea and food poisoning. Meningitis was another killer. As the lower-caste inhabitants in the village were mostly manual workers, they lived hand-to-mouth; given the absence of any medical facility, they had to go to nearby towns in search of treatment and this resulted sometimes in debts of up to fifty thousand rupees. Even their children weren't secure when the workers fell ill—they were left defenceless in their hovels. I was struck by the vikas mitr's undemonstrative, earnest tone. Only fifty yards away was the small hospital that my father had built in his mother's memory. I pointed at it. The vikas mitr didn't want to say anything that would offend me. Another man, now with a beard that had gone white, although I remembered him from earlier days when we had played in the village pond together, said that there was a hospital, sure, but there was no doctor and no access. He said, 'A fan is rotating inside, there is a bottle of water on the table, but there is a large lock hanging on the gate.'

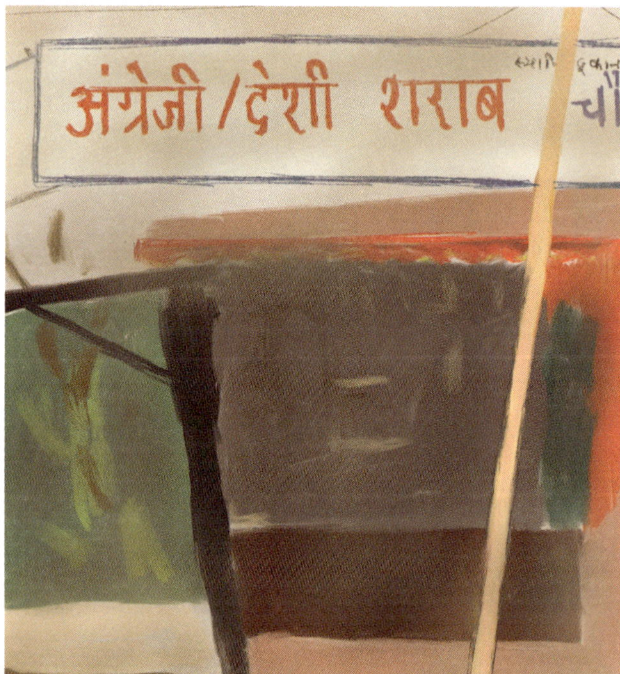

Particulate Matter, Delhi, 2022

December, 2022

The last time I was in Delhi it was hot. So hot that there were reports of overheated birds falling from the

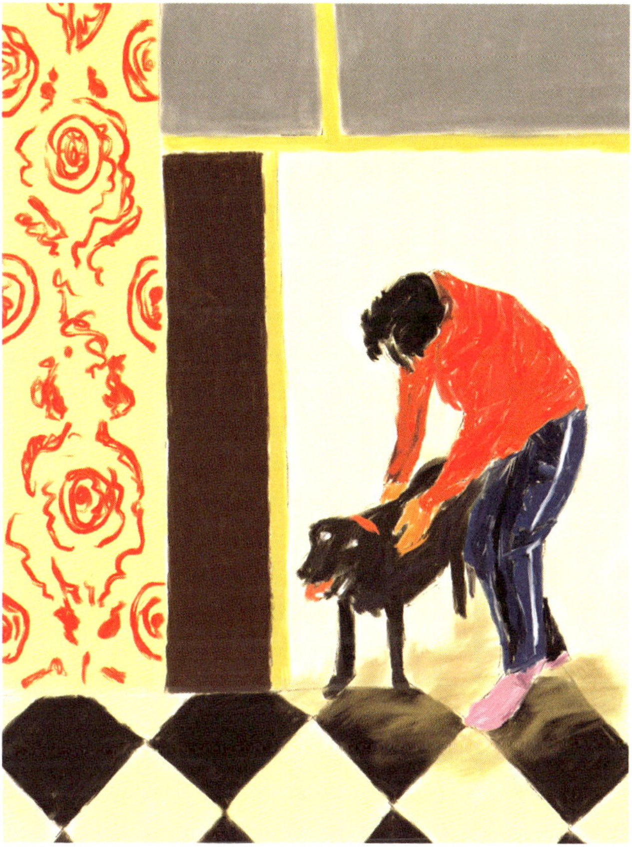

My Son with Neo, Delhi, 2023

sky. But now it was winter. It was foggy outside, the air smelling acrid. I had brought masks; they were no use. Very quickly I developed a sore throat and then a cough. When I complained about this to my publisher, he showed me a news item on his phone. 'Weather trends show capital no longer gets benign fog.' Delhi's air was described as carrying 'a large share of chlorides, sulphates and nitrates, and ions of calcium and ammonium'. I asked a friend of mine about the phrase 'particulate matter'—I had heard the term used to describe what gave the atmosphere its dark colour. My friend said it would be a good title for a Delhi painting.

When I had travelled to India last, I had been unable to get a visa for my son, because my wife was born in Pakistan. This time I had applied well in advance, and also appealed to a senior official in the foreign service who had been in high school with me. This time our luck held.

My father, eighty-seven now, was interested in showing my son our ancestral homestead. When we entered Jadopur, the placidity of the place reminded me of how much I missed it. When I visited the village as a schoolboy, I had always wanted to draw or photograph what I saw. My son got out of the car. Corn had been planted in one of our fields; the young plants were only ankle high. Several months ago, my father was told that someone else had ploughed the field. Another family in the village claimed that they had papers from the beginning of the last century showing ownership. This news had come as a blow to my father. My sister said that it left him disoriented. But then my father found the documents of sale that showed that the land had indeed been bought, back when he was a boy, from the family that was now claiming it.

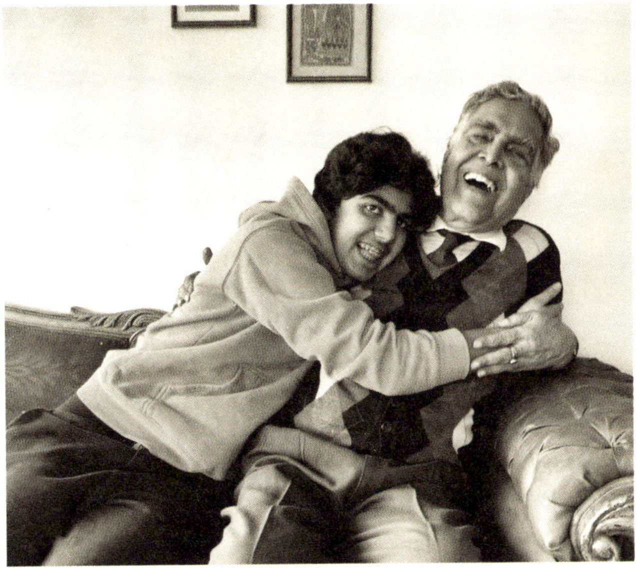

My Father with My Son Patna, Bihar, December 2022

I took my son on a walk to the village school that my father had built in my grandmother's memory. My father had been the first person in the entire district to be selected for the Indian Administrative Service; education had been his ticket out of the village. Most of his other relatives worked the land; a cousin became a doctor but others, if they left Jadopur, managed only to find low-paying jobs. When I was a child, my grandfather had been the village headman, but by the time I was in my teens power had shifted. My grandfather lost the panchayat election to a man from a lower caste. The family has little land remaining, but my father, perhaps because he feels he must give back what he owes to the land, has cultivated a philanthropic side.

At the school, boys were playing cricket. A middle-aged woman approached me. In a show of outdated modesty she had covered the lower part of her face, but I could see that she was smiling. She said that it was good I had come back, and then, pointing to a field close by, she said that a distant cousin of mine was now claiming that the land was his. I was taken aback. My relationship to the village was already tenuous, uncomfortably distant. Now it felt under threat. For decades, this land had been in the possession of my family. I didn't know what to say. I wasn't really back. I wasn't in a position to do anything. I was just visiting.

Mustard Fields, Jadopur, Bihar, December 2022

The thought came to me again. When my father was gone, a large part of my past would disappear, like one of those videos you see of landslides, an entire cliff

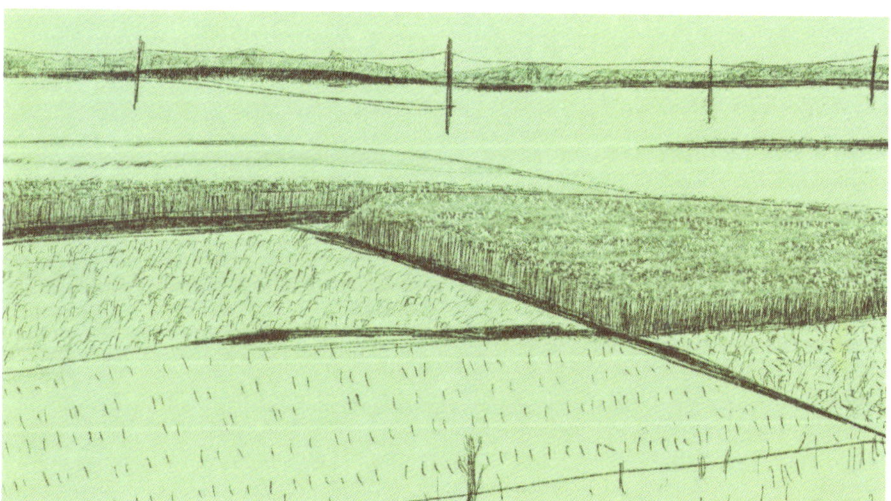

with a winding road and cars disappearing into the swirling river. It wasn't land or property that I was thinking about; I was thinking about my parents, my mother who had come to this village as a young bride, and my father, who had brought me today to the place where he had been born. It was the people who had made my past who would soon be gone.

The next day found me in quiet retreat, making a drawing of two adjacent mustard fields I had seen in the village. Is art a retreat from life and its contradictions? The answer would be yes. At least for me, that day. My eye had been attracted by the two intersecting lines of dense green topped by the bright yellow of the mustard, and now I felt compelled to render it all in a sombre monochrome.

I remembered both sides of that dirt road from my childhood, and the endless fields that stretched beyond. It was all very peaceful. Difficult to imagine, while looking at the small parcels of land with their neat rows of crops, all the battles over property waged within families and communities. As generations change, the plots are divided among siblings and grow smaller. There is less and less left to share. People leave for the cities. New buyers take over. This, at least, is what has happened in my village. My grandfather's land was divided between my father and his two brothers, but none of them live in the village. One of my uncles sold nearly all his land and moved to Bengaluru. I cannot imagine my own family's link to this rural place lasting beyond me. What I would like is for my father to sell his land during his lifetime, so that the new owners of the land will be from the village. Poorer families who couldn't simply up and move away. But why was it so hard to tell him this? To bring up the question of land, of inheritance?

Perhaps my father, too, in a far more real way than me, experienced the loss of his past. And he wasn't going to let it all disappear. He told me how he was a boy of eight or ten when he first saw an electric bulb. The world, and even his village, had changed so much during his long lifetime. He wasn't going to let me talk him out of the bit of land that had been the one stable corner of his life since his childhood.

When we were on our way back to Patna from the village, our car entered Motihari. This was the town where Gandhi had launched the satyagraha movement against the British. My son asked my father if he had memories of a childhood visit to Motihari. 'Yes,' my father said, 'I came here in 1944 to get my coat stitched.'

My father began to tell my son that in the year 1892, his great-grandfather Bhikhari Kuer had come to Champaran from Saran. As my father talked, I began to take notes. Bhikhari Kuer had five sons. His youngest son, Shrikrishna Kuer, had three sons, the youngest of whom, Amar Kuer, was my grandfather. I hadn't heard all the names of my ancestors that my father was reciting before now. Even as I was writing the names down, I realized that when my father was gone, no one would remember the details of our rural past. For my son's children, or his grandchildren, my father's name and, in time, my own name, might well be as remote to their lives as the name of my great-grandfather had become to mine. This wasn't a good or a bad thing; it was the way time worked. It also meant that the face I had seen on all the billboards in Delhi and in other cities—at the petrol station, on billboards at each street corner, in offices, in ads and in reports in every newspaper—wouldn't be around forever. And that, at least, gave me some comfort.

Bunches of Rasbhari, Patna, Bihar, 2023

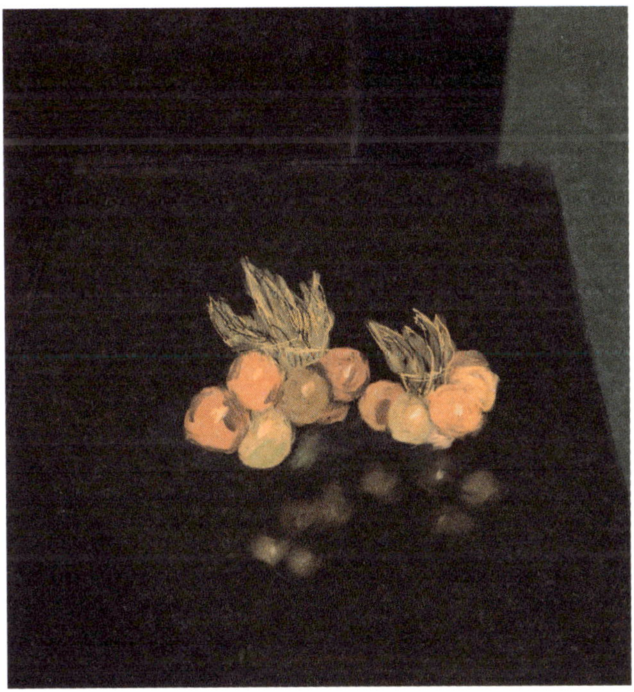

March, 2023

Patna. Each morning, for nearly ten days, I bought rasbhari from street vendors near my father's house. I was buying the fruit for my two sisters who were sitting vigil beside our father as he lay unconscious in a hospital at the other end of town. He was admitted to the hospital because he had been vomiting for a whole day. Once he was in the hospital, in a new, unexpected twist, his oxygen level began to plummet. My elder sister is a physician and she took the rational decision to have my father put on a ventilator. He was sedated and a tube inserted into his mouth to bring oxygen to his lungs. That same night, I bought a ticket for a flight from New York to Delhi and from there to Patna.

But my father didn't come out of the coma. What had happened to him, and that too so suddenly? Now and then his condition would improve, and then, inevitably, there would be a decline. One thing after another kept going wrong nearly every day. My birthday fell during this ordeal and my sisters, acting out of love and out of a desperate desire to think what my father would have liked, insisted that I cut a cake in the ICU. I have a photograph taken at midnight on my birthday. My sisters stand to my side. In front of me is a cake. And in the foreground on the hospital bed lies my comatose father with a tangle of tubes attached to him.

By the time he died, my father had been in the ICU for nearly a fortnight. My sisters usually spent the night at the hospital. I'd bring food each morning. For the first few days, I was reading a thousand-page-plus biography of Hanif Kureishi that I had promised to blurb; then, I began grading midterm papers that my students had submitted before leaving on their spring break. Several times a day I would make journal entries, even taking screenshots of what my sisters wrote on our shared WhatsApp group. As a result, I have a record of my father's rising or falling oxygen levels, his blood pressure, heart rate, amount of urine produced. What are these numbers but the repositories of our hopes and despair?

As a good dutiful Hindu son, I had only so far in my life touched my father's feet; our relationship had been somewhat formal. We had certainly never hugged the way my son and I often do. But now, in the ICU, I would hold my father's hand or caress his forehead with my palm in the hope that I was comforting him. The head doctor at the ICU encouraged us to speak to our father, assuring us that patients are sometimes able to hear even under sedation. My younger sister, an accomplished singer, sang all my father's favourite bhajans to him every day. I spoke to him in Bhojpuri, saying things like you will get better, everyone is here, do not lose courage, but also, in English, what I had never said to him before: I love you, thank you for everything you did for us, you showed us the way we ought to lead our lives. If his eyes moved, I'd begin

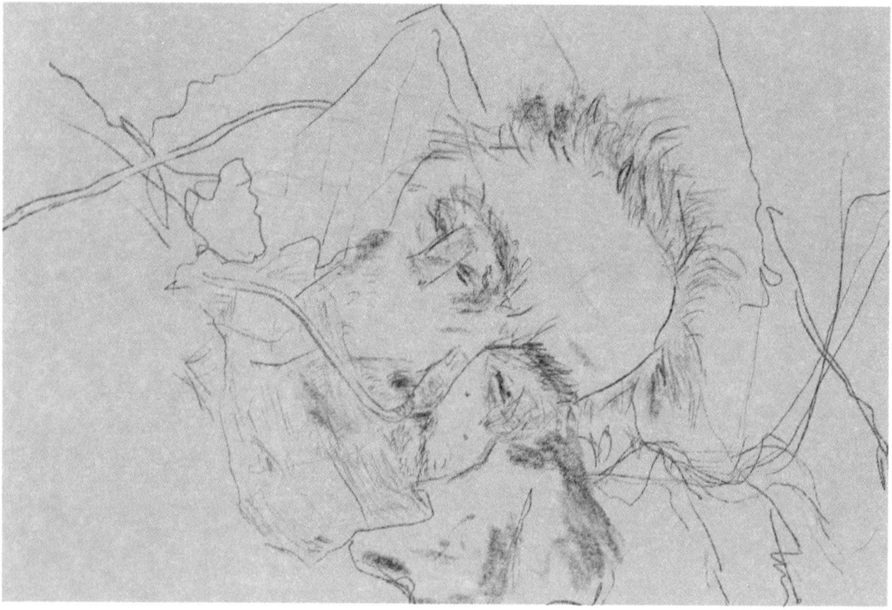

Pieces of Tape over My Father's Eyes and Nose, Patna, Bihar, 2023

speaking urgently. After I had said a word or two or three, my voice would rise with emotion and, despite the presence of a nurse or two in the room, I would often burst into tears.

A decision was taken by the doctors to put bits of tape over my father's eyelids. I cannot remember now whether this was because it was thought that the lights in the ceiling were hurting him or if it was because, unconscious though he was, his eyes never shut. A thin tube went into his body through the nose: this tube could be used to give him nutrition but was also used to suck out bile collecting in his stomach. The thick tube from the ventilator had turned my father's lips raw. The nurses sometimes put damp gauze on his mouth. His hair, darker than mine, had acquired an unkempt look. I was never as conscious of my mortality as when I looked at my handsome father's body in such a state of acute disrepair.

I wanted my father to wake up. If he opened his eyes, I would say to him that I had come home. If he stirred, I would tell him, even before he had opened his eyes, that I was standing close to him. That is how I had found him, one night in June 1975, the first night of Indira Gandhi's Emergency, when I had regained consciousness after having my tonsils removed. His voice had come to me in the dark: he was reciting for someone all the names of people thrown into prison.

No one lives forever. I wanted to tell my father to come back to us and stay around just a little longer. If he opened his eyes, I knew what to do: I would spread a towel under his chin and give him a fresh shave. Whenever I was coming to India and asked him what I could bring him, my father had always said, Nothing, just a few razors.

I had only once seen my father with a beard, when he had returned from the village after my grandfather's death. The shock of the white beard on him. Here at the hospital I'd pat his cheek with warm water, spread lather and use a new razor to scrape away with small, deft strokes all the days spent inside the ICU.

Enemy of the People

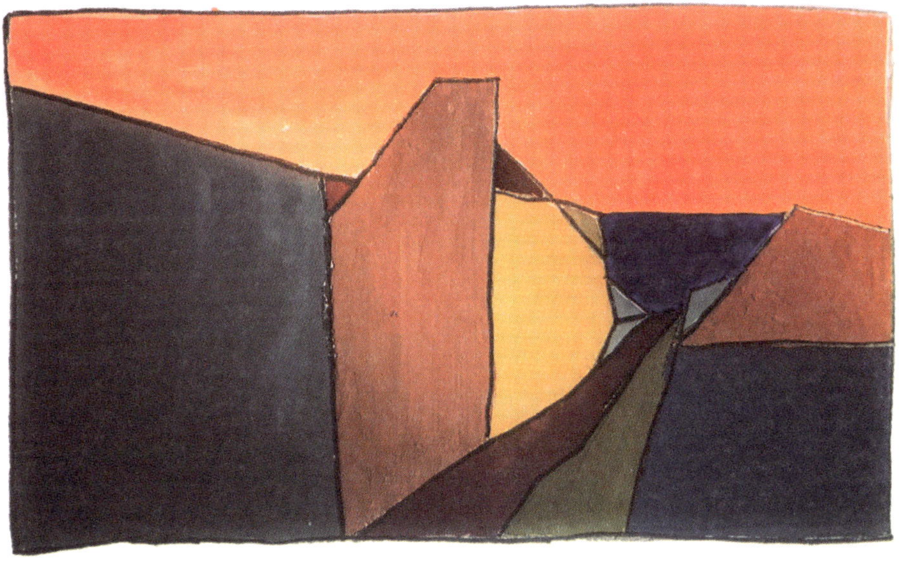

A Time Outside This Time #coronavirusdiary, Poughkeepsie, New York, 2020

For much of the Trump presidency, I had worked on a novel about the Trump presidency.

My protagonist, whom I had installed at an artist residency till a pandemic arrives, was writing a book titled 'Enemies of the People'. What held more than a little fascination for me was that a failed real estate mogul, a hustler who was also a sex offender, had to a large extent launched a political campaign with a lie about the then president's birthplace.

But the title of my protagonist's novel had to do with a different lie. Over and over, Trump would send out angry tweets calling journalists and news organizations enemies of the people. (For example, on 17 February 2019, Trump tweeted, in all caps: 'THE RIGGED AND CORRUPT MEDIA IS THE ENEMY OF THE PEOPLE'.) Op-eds reminded readers that Trump was repeating what Stalin had done to his opponents and the Nazis to Jews. Journalists pointed out that Trump's unhinged rants made their jobs not just difficult but also risky. I was born and had grown up in India, a country that has become among the most dangerous for journalists to work in, but I confess I wasn't thinking of attacks on journalists when I chose the title for my narrator's novel.

Instead, I was thinking of the comedian Sarah Silverman. Silverman, playing Trump's White House press secretary in the Hulu series *I Love You, America*, said: 'Don't be enemies of the people.' When I heard that, I felt that if all of us, writers and journalists, repeated Silverman's injunction, the charge would lose its sting and parody would win over propaganda.

The question that I was struggling with, and I hope it doesn't sound too grand when I put it this way, was how is art to respond to politics.

Unlike his predecessor, Trump was no reader. I knew he wouldn't have read the Norwegian playwright Henrik Ibsen's *An Enemy of the People* (1882). When I was finishing my novel, I read the play and then Arthur Miller's 1950 adaptation which, while retaining much of the original, makes the play more contemporary. Later, I also watched the great Indian director Satyajit Ray's film adaptation of the play, *Ganashatru* (1989). In Ibsen's play, a doctor in a town famous for its springs writes in the local paper that the waters are dangerously polluted. He is considered a public enemy for doing this, and he and his family are quickly made outcasts.

In the original play, and also in the adaptations which differ in important ways, one thing remains central: the doctor's belief that what is most necessary, and what will save us, is the ability to tell the truth in the newspapers. The idea of a robust public sphere, where reason and morality prevail, is the bedrock on which the doctor bases his resistance. Alas, the doctor's resistance doesn't succeed. He fails.

At the end of his play, Ibsen has the doctor declaring that he has made a discovery: 'It is this, let me tell you—that the strongest man in the world is he who stands most alone.'

There is a subtle shift in Arthur Miller's adaptation, a more modest articulation of faith. The emphasis now is not on strength but on loneliness. The doctor says at the end: 'You are fighting for the truth, and that's why you're alone. And that makes you strong. We're the strongest people in the world ... and the strong must learn to be lonely.'

By the play's end, the audience has learned with the doctor that it is naïve to believe that the truth is always recognized as truth. In fact, it is foolish to believe that the truth will even be allowed to be spoken or otherwise shared. The idea of an enlightened public sphere is a sham and entirely at the mercy of those in power.

The newspaper that had earlier courted the doctor and wanted to publish his protest reveals itself as craven, even mercenary. Which is all to say, Ibsen seems to be preaching exactly what Trump used to tweet. The media is the enemy of the people!

In *Ganashatru*, Satyajit Ray's film adaptation, there is an important departure from the earlier script. Prescient about the rise of Hindu majoritarianism and use of religion in Indian politics, the film shows the doctor discovering that contaminated water is being drunk at the temple where worshippers gather in large numbers.

In Ray's version, not everyone in the media is cowardly. A junior journalist working at the town's newspaper quits his job and resolves, as a freelancer, to interview the doctor and spread the news in the papers printed in the distant metropolis. He will also make sure, he says, that the doctor's report is published.

Delighted, the doctor tells the journalist that all he had ever wanted was 'to inform the people'. He offers that his article will be titled 'Confessions of an Enemy of the People'.

Not only that. In the film's closing scene, the members of the local theatre group and other educated liberals organize a march to support the doctor. We can hear the shouts ('Long live …'). And the doctor says: 'I am not alone. I may be an enemy of the people, but I have a lot of friends.'

Ray's is an altogether more hopeful ending, and one that at first disappointed me. I thought of all the activists and journalists that have been jailed ever since the Bharatiya Janata Party came to power, not to mention the legion of mainstream journalists

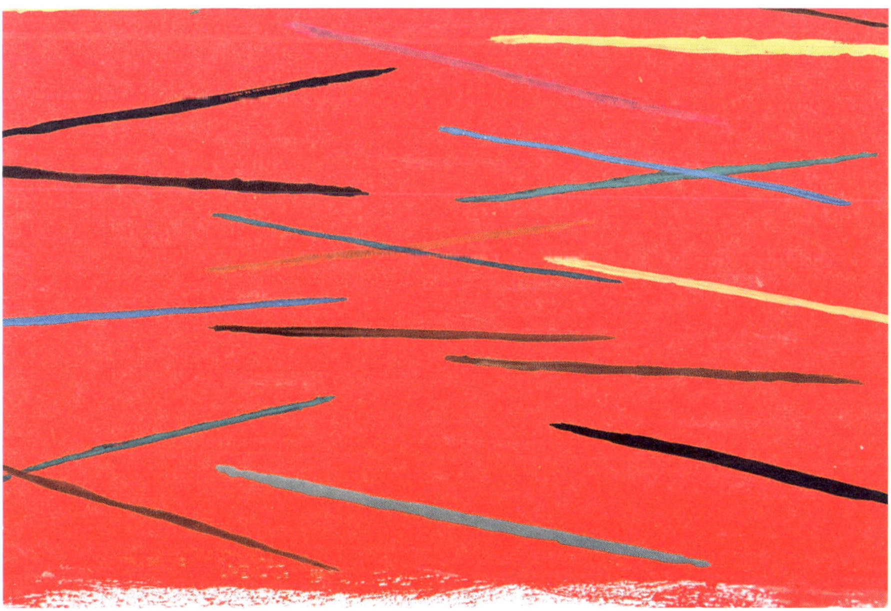

Indian Wins Gold in Tokyo Olympics, Poughkeepsie, New York, 2020

kowtowing to power, building a cult of personality around Modi.

At the same time, wasn't it also true that every recent repressive move by the government, and even every act of incivility or brutality, had been countered with the eruption of democratic, non-violent protests? Unlike Ibsen, Ray didn't want to show only the lonely individual raging against the machine; he wanted to portray local, resilient communities coming together to fight for their embattled truths.

I made the final changes in my novel in the days immediately after Trump's defeat in the election. For a while, and then for longer, it seemed that he wasn't going to accept that he had lost. The violent insurrection at the Capitol in Washington, DC showed that his followers were equally unlikely to admit the truth.

In those days of uncertainty and chaos, as I brought my novel to an end, what did I discover about art's relationship to politics? In the closing pages, my narrator is talking to a young man, a student, who has returned from a Black Lives Matter protest in upstate New York. In conversation via Zoom during the pandemic, they each begin to write down what they have experienced in recent days. What the two men, one young and the other old, are doing is bearing witness. They are trying to record their truth without being overwhelmed or defeated by it. Both are aware of the odds but what they also want to do, I think, is let their testimony reveal what is most dear to them, their precious humanity.

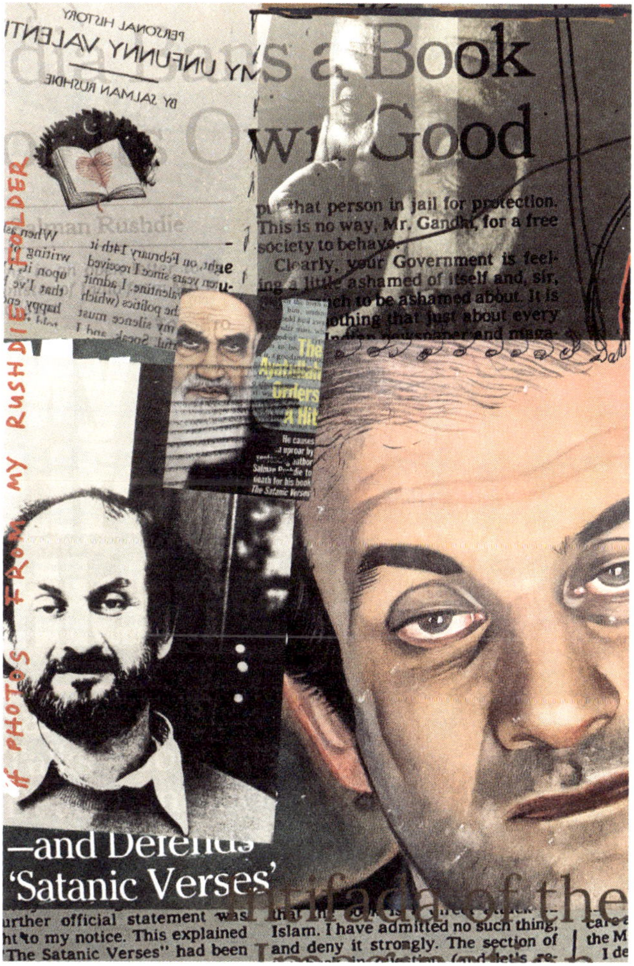

My Rushdie Folder from the 1980s–90s, 2022

Is Salman Rushdie an Enemy of the People?

In the opening paragraph of his memoir titled *Joseph Anton*, Rushdie writes about first receiving the call from a BBC reporter asking for a response to what had happened. 'How does it feel,' she asked him, 'to know that you have just been sentenced to death by the Ayatollah Khomeini?'

He remembers thinking, I'm a dead man.

But the expected didn't happen. Or not to him. His Japanese translator was killed. His Norwegian publisher was shot and his Italian translator knifed. Then, on an August morning in 2022, in upstate New York, just before a discussion about the United States serving as a refuge for writers, Rushdie was assaulted on stage by a twenty-four-year-old stranger wielding a knife. This savage attack, which inflicted grievous wounds but mercifully didn't prove fatal, had come thirty-three years after the fatwa.

In February 1989, the Ayatollah's act had introduced a new word, as Nobel laureate Nadine Gordimer noted, in the *Oxford Dictionary of New Words*: fatwa, 'originally a generic term for any legal decision' made by a religious authority 'but because of the particular context in which the West became familiar with the word, it is sometimes erroneously thought to mean "death sentence".'

After that first call from the BBC reporter, Rushdie thought he had only a few days to live, 'a single-digit number'. He left his home that day and didn't return till years later, when it was no longer his. He was required to have a code name so his cover wouldn't be blown. He chose Joseph Anton. (For all those years, a fictional name, a combination of the names of two writers he admired: Joseph Conrad and Anton Chekhov.) Policemen from the Special Branch guarded him round the clock. He spent nine years in hiding.

What were his days like? The novelist Peter Carey, in a letter written to mark a thousand days of Rushdie's exile, tried to imagine this life:

> [T]he fear, the loneliness of confronting your own face in God knows how many different mirrors in how many different safe houses, cleaning your teeth with a toothbrush a policeman has purchased for you, sleeping in strange beds with musty sheets, in old houses that make strange noises at night, new apartments with loud clocks, rattling refrigerators, heating that is too high or too low, and the distant voices of neighbours you will not meet.

This is what writers do, imagine other lives. Give voice to our experience and the experience of others on God's not-so-green-any-longer earth. When I was twenty-four, the same age as his assailant, Rushdie was magically imagining my life and making it real. Or so it felt. I was a new immigrant in the United

States, and in essay after essay, later collected in *Imaginary Homelands*, Rushdie offered me a language to recognize myself as an individual in the West. He had always asked: How does newness enter the world? It was a migrant's question. Rushdie also pitilessly excoriated the examples of Raj nostalgia being marketed in films and TV; I would hungrily watch those shows, but there was the writer teaching me how to view them in a political way. Against oversimplification and stereotyping, he emphasized complexity and history.

'Now of course *The Far Pavilions* is the purest bilge,' Rushdie wrote. 'The great processing machines of TV soap opera have taken the somewhat more fibrous garbage of the M.M. Kaye book and pureed it into easy-swallow, no-chewing-necessary drivel. Thus, the two central characters, both supposedly raised as Indians, have been lobotomized to the point of being incapable of pronouncing their own names.' In reading such lines dismissing 'a false Orient of cruel-lipped princes and the dusky slim-hipped maidens', I was attracted by the political stance, of course, but I was also stirred by the language itself. For me, a young man from a provincial town in India, to read Rushdie was to lose one's timidity when using English, the language of our former rulers. We could now declare our independence in the use of the language itself, flaunt it like he did, and suddenly appear bold and flamboyant.

Years passed. I also became a writer; it was the realization of a dream I had carried inside me for so long. At literary festivals, I would cross paths with Rushdie. We had our political differences, too, because we were changing, and so was the world around us. In 2012, en route to the Jaipur Literature Festival, I was excited to learn that I would see Rushdie there. But there was trouble. On my first day at the festival, the newspapers reported that hired assassins from the Mumbai underworld were on their way to assassinate Rushdie and that his visit had been called off. (The intelligence reports were later revealed to be fiction. Cops as magical realists.)

When the time came for my fellow writer Hari Kunzru and me to read from our works, we decided to protest Rushdie's absence by reading instead from *The Satanic Verses*, a book banned in India since its publication in 1988. The book was banned, yes, but we could download it on the internet. Our reading caused an immediate furore; the police arrived, and we were asked to leave the country. But what I want to say here is that I felt a great sense of freedom—a liberation from fear—as I read Rushdie's words out in public in the country of his birth.

All the inventiveness and joy of his fiction was there in the section of *The Satanic Verses* that I read out at the festival, when Gibreel Farishta considers the advantages of magically transforming London into a tropical city:

> Religious fervour, political ferment, renewal of interest in the intelligentsia. No more British reserve; hot-water bottles to be banished forever, replaced in the fetid nights by the making of slow and odorous love. Emergence of new social values: friends to commence dropping in on one another without making appointments, closure of old folks' homes, emphasis on the extended family. Spicier food; the use of water as well as paper in English toilets; the joy of running fully dressed through the first rains of the monsoon.

It had been important to do this, to remind readers of the pleasures of the book, even as outside there were calls for book burnings and the author's head.

Albert Camus believed that a writer's work is nothing but a slow trek to rediscover through the detours of art those two or three great and simple images in whose presence his or her heart first opened. The importance that Rushdie holds in our hearts—I mean here writers close to his age, like Hanif Kureishi, or like Kiran Desai, Raj Kamal Jha, Suketu Mehta, Ayad Akhtar, Téa Obreht and Zadie Smith from succeeding generations—is that there is a fundamental gesture or stance in our own writing that can be traced to what he accomplished in a book like *Midnight's Children*. What is true of writers is also, of course, true of readers: We all carry the memory of our encounters with books and their impress on our minds and our lives.

In my case, I have never forgotten Rushdie's declaration, back in the early 1980s, that 'the modern world lacks not only hiding places, but certainties'. He was saying there is no safe haven of religious belief or political quietism. Everything was open to question and revision. In his essay 'Outside the Whale', he declared, 'we are all irradiated by history, we are radioactive with history and politics; we see that it can be as false to create a politics-free fictional universe as to create one in which nobody needs to work or eat or hate or love or sleep.' I have found this credo inspiring when writing my fiction.

Has Hadi Matar, the young man who so cruelly stabbed Rushdie multiple times, ever read the man he attacked? Would he know that soon after the fatwa, in a short poem that Rushdie published in *Granta*, he wrote of wanting to 'sing on, in spite of attacks, / to sing (while my dreams are being murdered by facts) / praises of butterflies broken on racks'? That image of butterflies broken on instruments of torture is so striking and so powerful that I see at once why the great literary critic Edward Said once commented that Rushdie represented 'the intifada of the imagination'.

Ten years after the fatwa, in a piece in the *New Yorker* titled 'My Unfunny Valentine', Rushdie had stated that he was now going to write only of love. 'Love feels more and more like the only subject. At the centre of my life, of my new work, of my future plans, I now find nothing else.' When I re-read these words after Rushdie's stabbing, I thought of Hadi Matar in his jail cell. Acting in the spirit of Rushdie's words, I wanted to address Matar as a fellow human being and offer him an invitation, an invitation to read. I grew up in India's poorest state, and if I hadn't found the path of reading, I could have ended up being killed—or, pity the thought, a killer.

I wanted to say to Matar that like the man he tried to kill, I, too, am a writer. As my life has been given over to reading and writing books, I hold on to the belief that if we read widely and deeply, we will encounter people and places unlike ourselves. This sense of difference, its pleasures and challenges, will perhaps steer us away from intolerance. Many people in this country, including Malcolm X, discovered reading in prison—and were transformed. I hope that Matar, too, will find a similar liberation in learning.

One further point. In the days after the attack, we witnessed a universal outpouring of grief and concern for Rushdie. People were posting his lines on social media, they were discussing the influence of his work. Over the days that followed, I read nothing but his words in essays, novels and interviews. (My son, only twelve, declared his interest in reading *The Satanic Verses*. I told him that he should wait.) The reading we were doing had been a great consolation. Hadi Matar's attack failed—as any act of violence, and in such circumstances, inevitably would—because he had succeeded only in returning us to Rushdie's words. May literature live forever.

THEY WILL NOT COME BACK.

THOSE DAYS THAT WILL
NEVER COME BACK.
THEY WERE NEVER THERE.
THOSE DAYS THAT
WILL NOT COME BACK.

IN THE BAD NEW DAYS
YOU WILL FIND YOUR
BOLD NEW WAYS.

Letters to a Young Writer

These are letters that were never sent. In a way then they are for no one. And for everyone. I want to share my credos. In part, they are addressed to the academy. More precisely, to the pious, protective, self-serving language of academia. For instance, I don't know whether trigger warnings, and certainly the demand for trigger warnings, do the job that they are expected to do. I believe art should be honest, not tied to narcissism but turned outward to the world. It is a mistake to imagine that one becomes a writer by having a sharper sense of one's superiority or correctness. To write of this fallen world from a place of flawed awareness of the self and others—it is my belief that that is a preferable place for a writer to be. People at lit fests are always advising the young to be honest writers. But what does that even mean? Most of our leaders are clearly lying—they appear to be lying even to themselves. Don't do it. For me, honest writing is a writing that avoids an easy nostalgia and, more importantly, bad faith. To be honest means to work every day on one's themes and craft.

YOU ARE YOUNG
AND WHITE. YOU
HAVE READ BLUETS
AND HOLD ALL THE
RIGHT OPINIONS.
IT MUST BE NICE.

YOU LIKE AFFECT THEORY.
YOUR NEW POEMS
ARE ABOUT WHAT IT
MEANS TO WRITE
ETHICALLY ABOUT
THOSE WHO CAUSED
YOU TRAUMA. I LOVE
HOW PASSIVE-AGGRESSIVE
THAT IS. RESPECT!

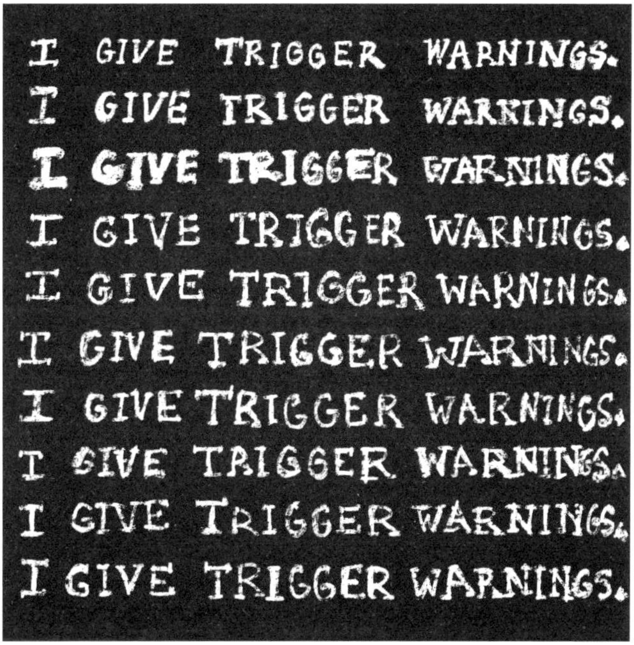
I GIVE TRIGGER WARNINGS.
I GIVE TRIGGER WARNINGS.
I GIVE TRIGGER WARNINGS.
I GIVE TRIGGER WARNINGS.
I GIVE TRIGGER WARNINGS.
I GIVE TRIGGER WARNINGS.
I GIVE TRIGGER WARNINGS.
I GIVE TRIGGER WARNINGS.
I GIVE TRIGGER WARNINGS.
I GIVE TRIGGER WARNINGS.

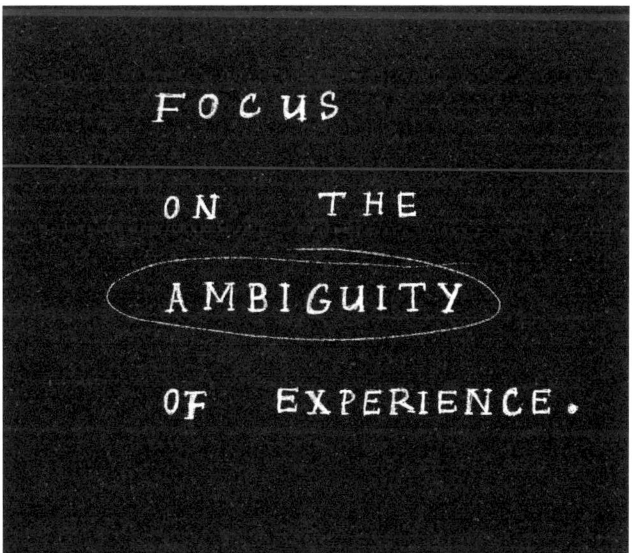
FOCUS
ON THE
AMBIGUITY
OF EXPERIENCE.

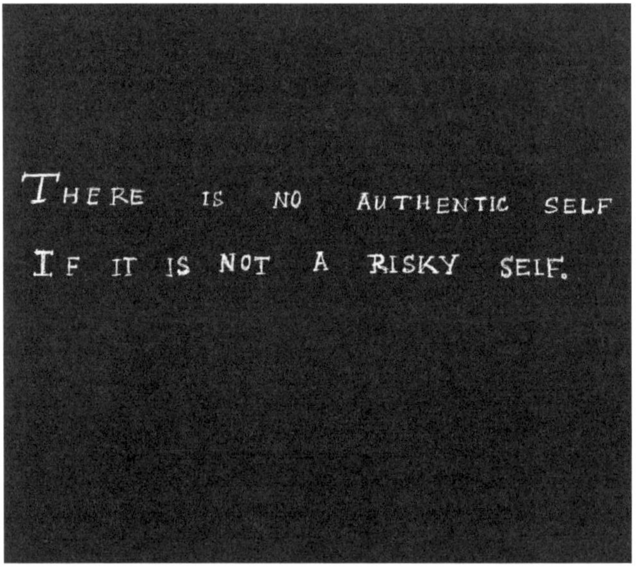
THERE IS NO AUTHENTIC SELF
IF IT IS NOT A RISKY SELF.

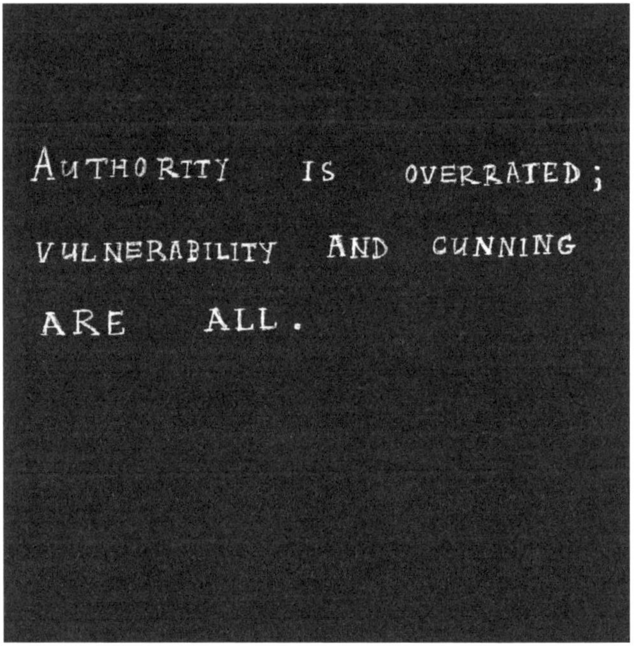
AUTHORITY IS OVERRATED;
VULNERABILITY AND CUNNING
ARE ALL.

GEORGIA O'KEEFFE WAS "AN ARTIST WHO SOUGHT TO CAPTURE NOT ONLY FORMS, BUT RHYTHM." WHEN I READ THAT I THOUGHT, YES! THAT IS WHAT ONE MUST DO WITH LANGUAGE!

OH VIRGINIA WOOLF,

WHERE ARE YOU?

Acknowledgements

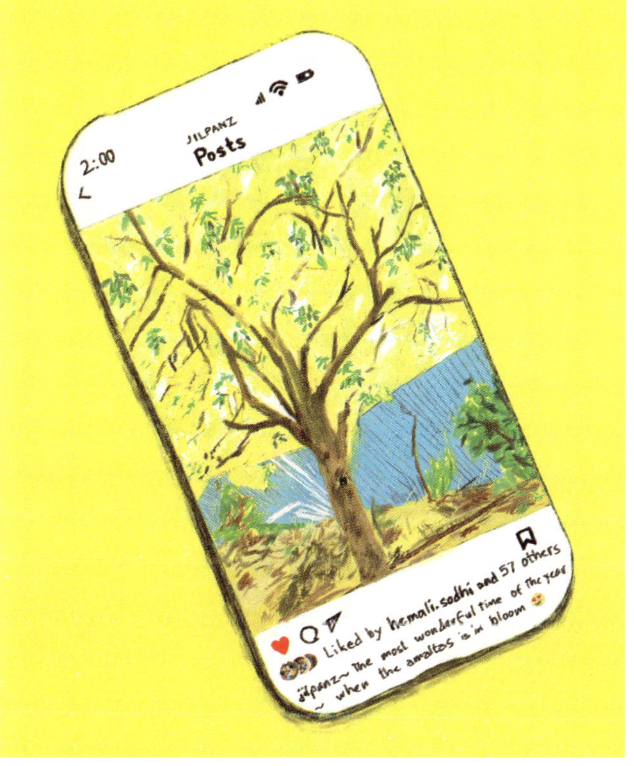

The essay 'Voice Lesson' is adapted from a craft-talk I gave at the Sewanee Writers' Conference in 2021. The drawings in the chapter, I made in Sewanee on small postcards that I mailed to friends. A longer version of this chapter has appeared in *Letters to a Writer of Color*, edited by Deepa Anappara and Taymour Soomro (New York: Random House, 2023). I have also drawn on two other pieces: 'Many Words for Heat, Many

Words for Hate', published in *Granta* 162 at the beginning of 2023, and 'Particulate Matter', published on Granta.com on 15 March 2023. I'm hugely indebted to my editor at *Granta*, Luke Neima, for his guidance and warmth.

I want to thank the Corporation of Yaddo where, in the comfort of Studio 1, Saratoga, I worked on the final version of this book.

When these diary entries were written, my friend Ian Jack hadn't died. In London, we had gone on walks together. Hanif Kureishi hadn't yet fallen down and been left paralysed. He hadn't yet dictated those sparkling reflections on illness and on writing that have inspired people all over the world. My father was still alive. The world turns and turns, again and again; I'm happy that a diary can serve as a record of changes and also as a memorial to what once was.

What hasn't changed is my gratitude to my agent Hemali Sodhi and my editor Udayan Mitra and the entire team at HarperCollins India, including Ananth Padmanabhan and Shatarupa Ghoshal. Thanks also to this book's designer, Gavin Morris. My love to Mona, Ila and Rahul, who have been my closest companions on this journey. My other fellow travellers will find themselves mentioned in these pages. To them I say that I trust there will be time to stop on yellow, even share a meal or raise a glass.

About the Author

Amitava Kumar is the author of several books of non-fiction and four novels. His work has appeared in *Granta*, the *New York Times*, *Harper's*, and several other publications. He has been awarded a Guggenheim fellowship and is currently a Cullman Center Fellow at the New York Library. His novel *Immigrant, Montana* was on the Best of the Year lists at the *New Yorker*, the *New York Times*, and Barack Obama's list of favourite books of 2018. His more recent novel *A Time Outside This Time* was described by the *New Yorker* as a 'shimmering assault on the Zeitgeist'. *My Beloved Life*, his latest novel, will be out soon. Kumar is professor of English at Vassar College in upstate New York.

HarperCollins *Publishers* India

At HarperCollins India, we believe in telling the best stories and finding the widest readership for our books in every format possible. We started publishing in 1992; a great deal has changed since then, but what has remained constant is the passion with which our authors write their books, the love with which readers receive them, and the sheer joy and excitement that we as publishers feel in being a part of the publishing process.

Over the years, we've had the pleasure of publishing some of the finest writing from the subcontinent and around the world, including several award-winning titles and some of the biggest bestsellers in India's publishing history. But nothing has meant more to us than the fact that millions of people have read the books we published, and that somewhere, a book of ours might have made a difference.

As we look to the future, we go back to that one word—a word which has been a driving force for us all these years.

Read.

Harper Collins

4th

HARPER PERENNIAL

HARPER BUSINESS

HARPER BLACK

हार्पर हिन्दी

HarperCollins *Children's Books*

HARPER DESIGN

HARPER VANTAGE

Harper Sport